I0813627

CROCHET AMIGURUMI FOR THE HOLIDAYS

CROCHET AMIGURUMI FOR THE HOLIDAYS

20+ FESTIVE CROCHET PROJECTS
FOR GIFTS, DECORATION, AND MORE

BIANCA SANTOS

weldonowen

To my husband, the patient keeper of yarn tangles, my steady hand on this creative journey, and the quiet strength behind every stitch—I love you.

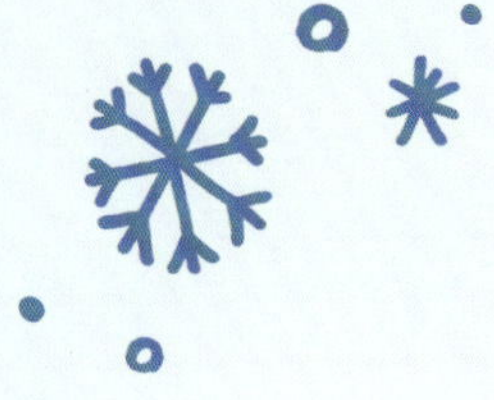
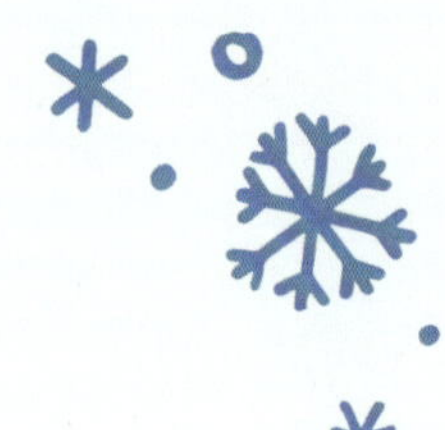

INTRODUCTION

Ever since I was a child, Christmas has been a special time for me. It was all about bringing the family together, cooking all day, sharing dinner, and exchanging gifts—our yearly tradition. But there was something missing. I grew up in Brazil, where Christmas happens in the summer, but I loved watching Christmas movies set in snowy cities, with a fireplace, North Pole animals, and a mug of hot cocoa. What better amigurumi collection to represent this cozy holiday season than the one created for this book?

Being an artist has always been a dream of mine. Since I was young, I've loved all kinds of crafts. I tried everything—embroidery, artistic calligraphy, you name it. I fell in love with every craft I tried, but crochet was the one that truly won my heart.

But my life hasn't always been about crafts. When I was eighteen, I joined the Air Force to become a sergeant. Over the thirteen years I served, I worked as an Air Traffic Controller and an Aviation English instructor and evaluator. Teaching has always been a great part of my life, alongside crafting.

I discovered amigurumi in 2015, and at first, it was just something to help me relax from my stressful job, but it quickly became an addiction! In 2020, I started creating my own patterns, driven by my love for creativity. It was during this time that I realized I wanted to pursue a dream of mine, so I moved to Finland and started working on my master's degree in education while working full time in my crochet business.

This book is a dream come true, combining my love for teaching, Christmas, and crochet. Every pattern here is made with care and love. Now it's your turn—grab your crochet hook, put on a Christmas playlist, and crochet your way through the best season of the year!

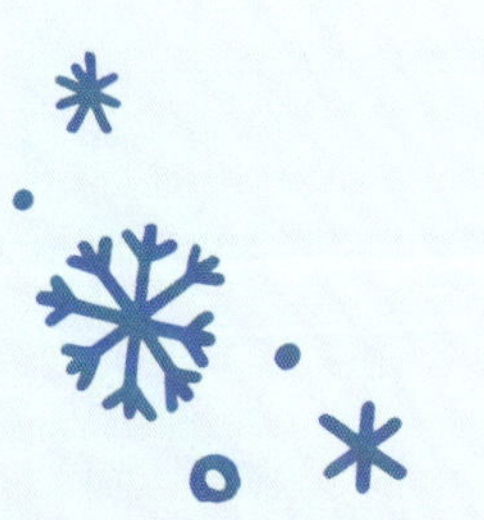
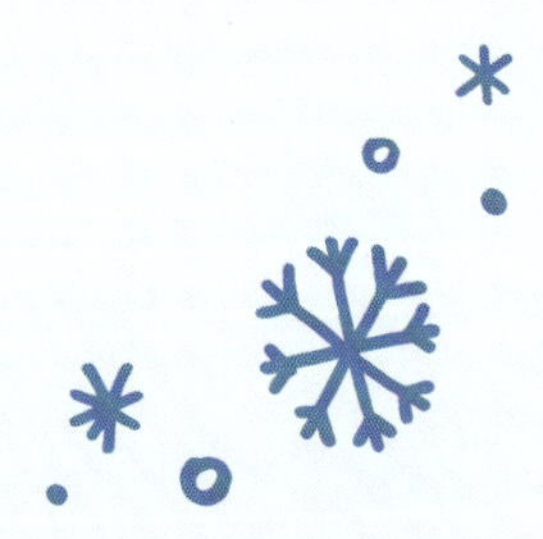

ORNAMENTS and DECORATION

CHRISTMAS STOCKING

There is nothing better than coming down the stairs on Christmas morning and finding your stocking stuffed with goodies. These stockings make wonderful ornaments or gift decorations, and can even be personalized!

YARN

1 skein of each of these colors:

Fingering weight (#1 super fine) yarn, shown in Hobbii *Friends Cotton 8/4* (100% cotton, 174 yd. / 160 m per 1.75 oz / 50 g skein)

MAIN COLOR

40 Tomato

87 Midnight Blue

SECONDARY COLOR

01 White

Lace yarn (#0 lace), shown in Hobbii *Rainbow Lace* (100% cotton, 306 yd. / 280 m per 1.75 oz / 50 g ball)

EMBROIDERY

01 White

FINISHED MEASUREMENTS

HEIGHT: 3.74 in. / 9.5 cm
WIDTH: 1.9 in. / 5 cm

HOOK

- US B-1 / 2.25 mm hook

NOTIONS

- Polyester stuffing
- Tapestry needle
- Removable stitch markers

GAUGE

Gauge is not critical for this project. Ensure your stitches are tight so the stuffing won't show through.

For more information on how to make the Stocking, including tips, step-by-step pictures, and videos, scan this QR code!

HEEL

With **White**, make a magic ring.
Rnd 1: 5 sc in ring, chain turn
Rnd 2: 1 inc, 3 sc, 1 inc, chain turn [7]
Rnd 3: 1 inc, 2 sc, 1 inc, 2 sc, 1 inc [10], chain turn
Rnd 4: (1 sc, 1 inc) x 5 [15], chain turn
Rnd 5: (4 sc, 1 inc) x 3 [18]
Now we have a semi-circle, and we will work on its flat part.
Make 1 inc, 8 sc, 1 inc [12]
Do not fasten off.

STOCKING

With **White**, make a magic ring.
Rnd 1: 6 sc in ring
Rnd 2: 6 inc [12]
Rnd 3: (1 sc, 1 inc) x 6 [18]
Rnd 4: 1 sc, 1 inc, (2 sc, 1 inc) x 5, 1 sc [24]
Rnd 5: (3 sc, 1 inc) x 6 [30]
Rnd 6: (9 sc, 1 inc) x 3 [33]
Rnd 7: 33 sc
Rnd 8: Change to **Tomato**, 33 sc
Rnds 9–12: 33 sc (4 rounds)
Rnd 13: 27 sc
Now we will join the Heel to the Stocking. Leave the **Tomato** yarn aside (do not fasten it off).
With **White**, start by crocheting the flat part of the semi-circle to the stocking. Hold the semi-circle in a way that you are able to make sc on both the flat part of the semi-circle, as well as the last round of the stocking itself.
Crochet 12 sc (passing through both the semi-circle and the stocking) and fasten off.
Now we will continue with **Tomato** yarn. The first st of the round will be on the first stitch of the Heel (in **White**).
Rnd 14: (11 sc, 1 dec) x 3 [36]
Rnd 15: 5 sc, 1 dec (10 sc) x 2, 5 sc [33]
Rnds 16–26: 33 sc (11 rounds)
Rnd 27: Change to **White**, 33 sc
Rnds 28–31: 33 sc (4 rounds)
Rnd 32: BLO (9 sc, 1 dec) x 3 [30]
Rnd 33: (1 sc, 1 dec) x 10 [20]
Rnd 34: 10 dec [10]

Stuff the Stocking as you crochet and close it with an inverted magic ring.

Insert the crochet hook in the front loops from round 32 and make:

Rnd 1–6: 33 sc (6 rounds)

Fasten off.

HANGER

With **White**, make 27 chains and from the second chain from the hook make 26 sc. Leave a long thread to sew.

With a tapestry needle, pass the two remaining threads of the chains (the thread that starts and ends the chains) on top of the inverted magic ring of the Stocking.

Pass the tapestry needle from the middle of the inverted magic ring to any point on the **white** top part of the Stocking.

Make the invisible knot and fasten off.

DECORATION

With **White #001**, work embroidery, making snowflakes or snowballs using French knots (see page 132) on your Stocking.

WINTER MITTENS

These cozy mittens evoke memories of playing in the snow, building snowmen, making snowballs, and sledding down your favorite hill, all while your hands are toasty warm. They make perfect ornaments, gift toppers, or even wreath decorations!

YARN

1 skein of each of these colors:

Fingering weight (#1 super fine) yarn, shown in Hobbii *Friends Cotton 8/4* (100% cotton, 174 yd. / 160 m per 1.75 oz / 50 g skein)

MAIN COLOR

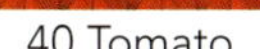

40 Tomato

87 Midnight Blue

SECONDARY COLOR

01 White

Lace yarn (#0 lace), shown in Hobbii *Rainbow Lace* (100% cotton, 306 yd. / 280 m per 1.75 oz / 50 g ball)

EMBROIDERY

01 White

FINISHED MEASUREMENTS

HEIGHT: 2.75 in. / 7 cm
WIDTH: 2.35 in. / 6 cm

HOOK

- US B-1 / 2.25 mm hook

NOTIONS

- Polyester stuffing
- Tapestry needle
- Removable stitch markers

GAUGE

Gauge is not critical for this project. Ensure your stitches are tight so the stuffing won't show through.

For more information on how to make the Mittens, including tips, step-by-step pictures, and videos, scan this QR code!

THUMB

With **Tomato**, make a magic ring.

Rnd 1: 6 sc in ring
Rnd 2: 6 inc [12]
Rnd 3: (5 sc, 1 inc) x 2 [14]
Rnds 4–8: 14 sc (5 rounds)
Fasten off.

MITTEN

With **Tomato**, make a magic ring.

Rnd 1: 6 sc in ring
Rnd 2: 6 inc [12]
Rnd 3: (1 sc, 1 inc) x 6 [18]
Rnd 4: 1 sc, 1 inc, (2 sc, 1 inc) x 5, 1 sc [24]
Rnd 5: (3 sc, 1 inc) x 6 [30]
Rnd 6: (9 sc, 1 inc) x 3 [33]
Rnds 7–14: 33 sc (8 rounds)
Place the Thumb next to the Mitten. On round 15, we will crochet 7 sc (half of the Thumb) and in round 16 we will crochet the second half of the Thumb. That way, we will have the Thumb crocheted with the Mitten, without sewing.
Rnd 15: 7 sc joining half of the Thumb to the Mitten (these 7 sc are both on the Thumb and on the Mitten at the same time), 26 sc [33]
Rnd 16: 7 sc joining the other half of the Thumb to the Mitten (these 7 sc are both on the Thumb and on the Mitten at the same time), 26 sc [33]
Rnds 17–20: 33 sc (4 rounds)
Change to **White**
Rnds 21–24: 33 sc (4 rounds)
Rnd 25: BLO (9 sc, 1 dec) x 3 [30]
Rnd 26: (1 sc, 1 dec) x 10 [20]
Rnd 27: 10 dec [10]
Stuff the Mitten as you crochet and close it with an inverted magic ring.

Insert the crochet hook in the front loops from round 25 and make:
Rnds 1–5: 33 sc (5 rounds)
Fasten off.

HANGER

With **White** make 27 chains and from the second chain from the hook make 26 sc. Leave a long thread to sew.
With a tapestry needle, pass the two remaining threads of the chains (the thread that starts and ends the chains) on top of the inverted magic ring of the Mitten.
Pass the tapestry needle from the middle of the inverted magic ring to any point on the **White** top part of the Mitten.
Make the invisible knot and fasten off.

DECORATION

With **White #001**, work embroidery, making snowflakes or snowballs using French knots (see page 132) on your Mittens.

BALL ORNAMENTS

These ornaments are perfect for the beginning stitcher, and are so versatile—you can make them in any color you like, and even personalize them, making them a treasured heirloom for years to come.

YARN

1 skein of each of these colors:

Fingering weight (#1 super fine) yarn, shown in Hobbii *Friends Cotton 8/4* (100% cotton, 174 yd. / 160 m per 1.75 oz / 50 g skein)

BALLS

28 Mustard

82 Prussian Blue

112 Bottle Green

Fingering weight (#1 super fine) yarn, shown in Hobbii *Friends Cotton 8/4* (100% cotton, 174 yd. / 160 m per 1.75 oz / 50 g)

17 Cognac

48 Dark Magenta

Lace yarn (#0 lace), shown in Hobbii *Rainbow Lace* (100% cotton, 306 yd. / 280 m per 1.75 oz / 50 g ball)

EMBROIDERY

01 White

FINISHED MEASUREMENTS

HEIGHT: 2.15 in. / 5.5 cm

HOOK

- US B-1 / 2.25 mm hook

NOTIONS

- Polyester stuffing
- Tapestry needle
- Removable stitch markers
- Tweezers

GAUGE

Gauge is not critical for this project. Ensure your stitches are tight so the stuffing won't show through.

For more information on how to make the Ornaments, including tips, step-by-step pictures, and videos, scan this QR code!

BALL

With **Prussian Blue**, **Bottle Green**, **Dark Magenta** or **Cognac**, make a magic ring.

Rnd 1: 6 sc in ring

Rnd 2: 6 inc [12]

Rnd 3: (1 sc, 1 inc) x 6 [18]

Rnd 4: 1 sc, 1 inc, (2 sc, 1 inc) x 5, 1 sc [24]

Rnd 5: (3 sc, 1 inc) x 6 [30]

Rnd 6: 2 sc, 1 inc, (4 sc, 1 inc) x 5, 2 sc [36]

Rnd 7: (5 sc, 1 inc) x 6 [42]

Rnd 8: 3 sc, 1 inc, (6 sc, 1 inc) x 5, 3 sc [48]

Rnds 9–16: 48 sc (8 rounds)

Rnd 17: 3 sc, 1 dec, (6 sc, 1 dec) x 5, 3 sc [42]

Rnd 18: (5 sc, 1 dec) x 6 [36]

Rnd 19: 2 sc, 1 dec, (4 sc, 1 dec) x 5, 2 sc [30]

Rnd 20: (3 sc, 1 dec) x 6 [24]

Rnd 21: 1 sc, 1 dec, (2 sc, 1 dec) x 5, 1 sc [18]

Rnd 22: BLO (1 sc, 1 dec) x 6 [12]

Rnd 23: 6 dec [6]

Stuff the Ball as you crochet and fasten it off with an inverted magic ring.

Insert the hook in the loops formed by round 22.

With **Mustard**.

Rnd 1: 18 sl st

Rnd 2: BLO 18 sc

Rnd 3: 18 sc

Rnd 4: BLO (1 sc, 1 dec) x 6 [12]

Rnd 5: 6 dec [6]

Stuff this part and close it with an inverted magic ring.

HANGER

With **Mustard**, make 26 chains and leave a long thread.

With a tapestry needle, pass the remaining thread through the middle of the magic ring. Pass the other end of the thread in the middle of the magic ring too.

Tie a knot with the remaining threads and fasten off.

DECORATION

Decorate your Christmas Balls using **White #001** for embroidery. You can decorate them with snowflakes, a Christmas tree, or use French knots (see page 132) to make smaller snowflakes.

CANDY CANE

Is there any sweeter treat for the holidays than a candy cane? These candy canes may not be tasty, but they would look sweet hanging on the tree, or as part of a handmade present!

YARN

1 skein of each of these colors:

Fingering weight (#1 super fine), shown in Hobbii *Friends Cotton 8/4* (100% cotton, 174 yd. / 160 m per 1.75 oz / 50 g skein).

01 White

40 Tomato

FINISHED MEASUREMENTS

HEIGHT: 3.15 in. / 8 cm

HOOK

- US B-1 / 2.25 mm hook

NOTIONS

- Tapestry needle
- Removable stitch markers
- Pipe cleaner

GAUGE

Gauge is not critical for this project. Ensure your stitches are tight so the stuffing won't show through.

For more information on how to make the Candy Cane, including tips, step-by-step pictures, and videos, scan this QR code!

With **White**, make a magic ring.

From round 3 on we will start making color changes to **Tomato**. The color you work with is indicated before each part.

Rnd 1: 6 sc in ring

Rnd 2: (1 sc, 1 inc) x 3 [9]

Rnd 3: (**White**) 1 sc, (**Tomato**) 2 sc, (**White**) 2 sc, (**Tomato**) 2 sc, 2 sc [9]

Rnd 4: (**Tomato**) 2 sc, (**White**) 2 sc, (**Tomato**) 2 sc, (**White**) 2 sc, (**Tomato**) 1 sc [9]

Rnd 5: (**Tomato**) 1 sc, (**White**) 2 sc, (**Tomato**) 2 sc, (**White**) 2 sc, (**Tomato**) 2 sc [9]

Rnd 6: (**White**) 2 sc, (**Tomato**) 2 sc, (**White**) 2 sc, (**Tomato**) 2 sc, (**White**) 1 sc [9]

Repeat the sequence from rounds 3 to 6 for 8 times. If you want a longer cane, you can repeat this sequence more times. Mark the beginning of each round to make it easier to follow. Another option is just keep changing colors every 2 stitches until you get to a desired size.

For the last round, keep the **Tomato** color and make:

(1 sc, 1 dec) x 3 [6]

Insert the pipe cleaner inside the Candy Cane and close it with an inverted magic ring. Do not stuff it.

Bend the tip of the piece to shape the Candy Cane.

CHRISTMAS TREE

Decorating the tree has always been one of my favorite holiday activities. Here, you can decorate your tree any way you wish—or make several and create your own winter wonderland!

YARN

1 skein of each of these colors:

Fingering weight (#1 super fine) yarn, shown in Hobbii *Friends Cotton 8/4* (100% cotton, 174 yd. / 160 m per 1.75 oz / 50 g skein)

POT

13 Ochre

Fingering weight (#1 super fine) yarn, shown in Hobbii *Friends Cotton 8/4 Mercerized* (100% cotton, 174 yd. / 160 m per 1.75 oz / 50 g skein)

LACE

40 Tomato

TREE

112 Bottle Green

TREE TRUNK

12 Chocolate

Fingering weight (#1 super fine) yarn, Hobbii *Tencel Bamboo Fine* (40% Tencel, 60% bamboo viscose, 230 yd. / 210 m per 1.8 oz / 50 g skein)

STAR

17473 Curry

FINISHED MEASUREMENTS

HEIGHT: 7.5 in. / 19 cm

WIDTH: 2.75 in. / 7 cm

HOOK

- US B-1 / 2.25 mm hook

NOTIONS

- Polyester stuffing
- Tapestry needle
- Removable stitch markers
- Straight pins
- Beads
- Cardboard

GAUGE

Gauge is not critical for this project. Ensure your stitches are tight so the stuffing won't show through.

For more information on how to make the Tree, including tips, step-by-step pictures, and videos, scan this QR code!

POT

With **Ochre**, make a magic ring.
Rnd 1: 8 sc in ring
Rnd 2: 8 inc [16]
Rnd 3: (1 sc, 1 inc) x 8 [24]
Rnd 4: 1 sc, 1 inc, (2 sc, 1 inc) x 7, 1 sc [32]
Rnd 5: (3 sc, 1 inc) x 8 [40]
Rnd 6: 2 sc, 1 inc, (4 sc, 1 inc) x 7, 2 sc [48]
Rnd 7: BLO 48 sc
Rnd 8: (5 sc, 1 inc) x 8 [56]
Rnd 9: 56 sc
Rnd 10: 3 sc, 1 inc, (6 sc, 1 inc) x 7, 3 sc [64]
Rnds 11–18: 64 sc (8 rounds)
Rnd 19: 3 sc, 1 dec, (6 sc, 1 dec) x 7, 3 sc [56]
Rnd 20: FLO (4 sc, make 3 chains and skip 3 sc) repeat 8 times [56]
Rnd 21: (4 sc, 4 hdc inside the hole) x 8 [64]
Fasten off.
Put a piece of cardboard to the base to make the base of the Pot flat.
Insert the crochet hook in the first loop formed in round 20.
With **Chocolate**:
Rnd 1: 56 sc
Rnd 2: (5 sc, 1 dec) x 8 [48]
Rnd 3: 2 sc, 1 dec, (4 sc, 1 dec) x 7, 2 sc [40]
Rnd 4: 1 sc, 1 dec, (2 sc, 1 dec) x 9, 1 sc [30]
Rnd 5: FLO 30 sc
Rnds 6–11: 30 sc (6 rounds)
Rnd 12: Change to **Bottle Green**. FLO 30 sl st.
Rnd 13: BLO 1 sc, 1 inc, (2 sc, 1 inc) x 9, 1 sc [40]
Rnd 14: (3 sc, 1 inc) x 10 [50]
Rnd 15: 2 sc, 1 inc, (4 sc, 1 inc) x 9, 2 sc [60]
Rnd 16: (11 sc, 1 inc) x 5 [65]
Rnd 17: 6 sc, 1 inc, (12 sc, 1 inc) x 4, 6 sc [70]
Rnd 18: (13 sc, 1 inc) x 5 [75]
Fasten off.
Cut a round piece of cardboard and glue on the base of the Tree to keep it flat. Make sure that there is no glue on round 18 because we are going to crochet the Tree to that part.

TREE

With **Bottle Green**, make a magic ring.
Rnd 1: 6 sc in ring
Rnd 2: (1 sc, 1 inc) x 3 [9]
Rnd 3: 1 sc, 1 inc, (2 sc, 1 inc) x 2, 1 sc [12]
Rnd 4: (3 sc, 1 inc) x 3 [15]
Rnd 5: 2 sc, 1 inc, (4 sc, 1 inc) x 2, 2 sc [18]
Rnd 6: (5 sc, 1 inc) x 3 [21]
Rnd 7: 3 sc, 1 inc, (6 sc, 1 inc) x 2, 3 sc [24]
Rnd 8: (7 sc, 1 inc) x 3 [27]
Rnd 9: 4 sc, 1 inc, (8 sc, 1 inc) x 2, 4 sc [30]
Rnd 10: (9 sc, 1 inc) x 3 [33]
Rnd 11: 5 sc, 1 inc, (10 sc, 1 inc) x 2, 5 sc [36]
Rnd 12: BPsc 36
Rnd 13: 1 sc, 1 dec, (2 sc, 1 dec) x 8, 1 sc [27]
Rnd 14: FLO 4 sc, 1 inc, (8 sc, 1 inc) x 2, 4 sc [30]

Rnd 15: 2 sc, 1 inc, (4 sc, 1 inc) x 5, 2 sc [36]
Rnd 16: (11 sc, 1 inc) x 3 [39]
Rnd 17: 6 sc, 1 inc, (12 sc, 1 inc) x 2, 6 sc [42]
Rnd 18: (13 sc, 1 inc) x 3 [45]
Rnd 19: 7 sc, 1 inc, (14 sc, 1 inc) x 2, 7 sc [48]
Rnd 20: 48 sc
Rnd 21: (15 sc, 1 inc) x 3 [51]
Rnd 22: 51 sc
Rnd 23: 8 sc, 1 inc, (16 sc, 1 inc) x 2, 8 sc [54]
Rnd 24: BPsc 54
Rnd 25: 2 sc, 1 dec, (4 sc, 1 dec) x 2, 2 sc [45]
Rnd 26: FLO 7 sc, 1 inc, (14 sc, 1 inc) x 2, 7 sc [48]
Rnd 27: (7 sc, 1 inc) x 6 [54]
Rnd 28: (17 sc, 1 inc) x 3 [57]
Rnd 29: 9 sc, 1 inc, (18 sc, 1 inc) x 2, 9 sc [60]
Rnd 30: (19 sc, 1 inc) x 3 [63]
Rnd 31: 10 sc, 1 inc, (20 sc, 1 inc) x 2, 10 sc [66]
Rnd 32: (21 sc, 1 inc) x 3 [69]
Rnd 33: 11 sc, 1 inc, (22 sc, 1 inc) x 2, 11 sc [72]
Rnd 34: (23 sc, 1 inc) x 3 [75]
Rnd 35: 75 sc
Crochet the Tree to the base with the Pot. Crochet 75 sc to join both parts together. Stuff as you close it.

STAR

With **Curry**, make a magic ring.
Chain 2 and make 15 hdc inside the magic ring. Pull the yarn to close the ring tightly.
Insert the hook into the second chain from the start and make a slip stitch to close the round.
To create the points of the star: Chain 5.
Starting from the second chain from the hook: 1 sc, 1 hdc, 1 dc, 1 tr.
Skip 2 stitches in the round and make a slip stitch into the third stitch.
Repeat this step 4 times for a total of 5 points on the star. After completing the final tip of the star, sl st into the third stitch (as before), cut the yarn and fasten off, leaving a piece of thread to sew it on the top of the tree.

LACE

With **Tomato**.
Make 80 chains and fasten off. Pass the Lace in zigzag in the holes created in the Pot and tie Lace in a bow to finish.
Decorate your Tree with Beads as desired.

STAR ORNAMENT

This star may not twinkle, but it can be the centerpiece for your Christmas.

YARN

Fingering weight (#1 super fine) yarn, shown in Hobbii *Friends Cotton 8/4* (100% cotton, 174 yd. / 160 m per 1.75 oz / 50g)

28 Mustard

Fingering weight (#1 super fine) yarn, shown in Hobbii *Friends Cotton 8/4 Mercerized* (100% cotton, 174 yd. / 160 m per 1.75 oz / 50g)

26 Dark Yellow

FINISHED MEASUREMENTS

HEIGHT: 2.35 in. / 6 cm

WIDTH: 2.35 in. / 6 cm

HOOK

- US B-1 / 2.25 mm hook

NOTIONS

- Polyester stuffing
- Tapestry needle
- Removable stitch markers

GAUGE

Gauge is not critical for this project. Ensure your stitches are tight so the stuffing won't show through.

For more information on how to make the Star, including tips, step-by-step pictures, and videos, scan this QR code!

STAR

Rnd 1: 6 sc in magic ring
Rnd 2: 6 inc [12]
Rnd 3: (1 sc, 1 inc) x 6 [18]
Rnd 4: 1 sc, 1 inc, (2 sc, 1 inc) x 5, 1 sc [24]
Rnd 5: (3 sc, 1 inc) x 6 [30]
Fasten off the first piece and make another one, from rounds 1 to 5.
Place both parts together and make 1 sc. This will be the first st of one tip of the Star.
When joining both parts together, pay attention to having the right side of the amigurumi out!
We will make 5 times the sequence below to make the tip of the Star.

THE FIRST TIP OF THE STAR

Rnd 1: 1 sc joining the second to the first piece, 5 sc in the first piece,
Count 6 stitches to the first one
1 sc joining the first piece to the second, 5 sc in the second piece [12]
We will now work in continuous rounds:
Rnd 2: (4 sc, 1 dec) x 2 [10]
Rnd 3: 10 sc
Rnd 4: (3 sc, 1 dec) x 2 [8]
Rnd 5: (2 sc, 1 dec) x 2 [6]
Fasten off with an inverted magic ring.
Start again.
Rnd 1: Insert the crochet hook in the first st next to the tip of the star. Make 6 sc, count 6 st far from the tip of the star at the other side of the crochet piece, and make 1 sc joining both parts + 5 sc [12]
Rnd 2: (4 sc, 1 dec) x 2 [10]
Rnd 3: 10 sc
Rnd 4: (3 sc, 1 dec) x 2 [8]
Rnd 5: (2 sc, 1 dec) x 2 [6]
Stuff the tips of the stars as you finish them. Use tweezers to continue stuffing the last tip of the star. With the remaining thread of the last tip of the star, close the gaps between each tip of the star and fasten off.

HOLLY BELL

Whether it's decorating the tree, your house, or your gifts, this crocheted bell with holly leaves and berries is the perfect holiday accent. It even has a jingle bell for a clapper, so you can truly ring in the season.

YARN

1 skein of each of these colors:

Fingering weight (#1 super fine) yarn, shown in Hobbii *Friends Cotton 8/4 Mercerized* (100% cotton, 174 yd. / 160 m per 1.75 oz / 50 g skein).

BELL

26 Dark Yellow

HOLLY BERRY

40 Tomato

HOLLY LEAF

112 Bottle Green

FINISHED MEASUREMENTS

HEIGHT: 2.35 in. / 6 cm

WIDTH: 2.35 in. / 6 cm

HOOK

- US B-1 / 2.25 mm hook

NOTIONS

- Polyester stuffing
- Tapestry needle
- Removable stitch markers
- Small bell for clapper

GAUGE

Gauge is not critical for this project. Ensure your stitches are tight so the stuffing won't show through.

For more information on how to make the Bell, including tips, step-by-step pictures, and videos, scan this QR code!

BELL

With **Dark Yellow**, make a magic ring.
Rnd 1: 8 sc in ring
Rnd 2: 8 inc [16]
Rnd 3: (1 sc, 1 inc) x 8 [24]
Rnd 4: 1 sc, 1 inc, (2 sc, 1 inc) x 8 [32]
Rnds 5–6: 32 (2 rounds)
Rnd 7: (3 sc, 1 dec) x 8 [40]
Rnds 8–10: 40 (3 rounds)
Rnd 11: (7 sc, 1 inc) x 5 [45]
Rnd 12–13: 45 sc (2 rounds)
Rnd 14: 4 sc, 1 inc, (8 sc, 1 inc) x 4, 4 sc [50]
Rnds 15–16: 50 sc (2 rounds)
Rnd 17: 2 sc, 1 inc, (4 sc, 1 inc) x 9, 2 sc [60]
Rnd 18: 60 sc
Rnd 19: (1 chain, 1 sl st) x 60 [60]
Fasten off.
With **Dark Yellow** make 30 chains and leave a long thread to sew. Pass the cord with chains inside the small Bell. Using the tapestry needle pass the remaining thread from the inside of the Bell to the outside through the magic ring. Tie a knot and fasten off.

HOLLY LEAF (MAKE TWO)

With **Bottle Green**.
Start with 25 chains, and from the second chain from the hook.
Make:
(1 sl st, 1 sc, 1 hdc, 6 dc, 1 hdc, 1 sc, 1 sl st) x 2
Make 2 chains and now we will work on the opposite side of the chains.
(1 sl st, 1 sc, 1 hdc, 6 dc, 1 hdc, 1 sc, 1 sl st) x 2 [52]
Make 2 chains and close it with 1 sl st in the first stitch of the crochet piece. This is the first st of the round!
3 sl st, (1 sc, 1 hdc, 1 chain, 1 sc inside the hdc, 1 sc), 3 sl st, (1 sc, 1 hdc, 1 chain, 1 sc inside the hdc, 1 sc), 8 sl st, (1 sc, 1 hdc, 1 chain, 1 sc inside the hdc, 1 sc), 3 sl st, (1 sc, 1 hdc, 1 chain, 1 sc inside the hdc, 1 sc), 4 sl st, 1 chain, 4 sl st,
(1 sc, 1 hdc, 1 chain, 1 sc inside the hdc, 1 sc), 3 sl st, (1 sc, 1 hdc, 1 chain, 1 sc inside the hdc, 1 sc), 8 sl st, (1 sc, 1 hdc, 1 chain, 1 sc inside the hdc, 1 sc), 3 sl st, (1 sc, 1 hdc, 1 chain, 1 sc inside the hdc, 1 sc), 3 sl st, 1 chain, 1 sl st.

HOLLY BERRY (MAKE TWO)

With **Tomato**, make a magic ring.
Rnd 1: 6 sc in ring
Rnd 2: 6 inc [12]
Rnd 3: (1 sc, 1 inc) x 6 [18]
Rnds 4–6: 18 sc (3 rounds)
Rnd 7: (1 sc, 1 dec) x 6 [12]
Rnd 8: 6 dec [6]
Stuff the Holly Berry and close it with an inverted magic ring. Leave a long thread to sew.

ASSEMBLY

Glue the Leaves on top of the Bell.
Glue both Berries on top of the Leaves or sew them if you prefer.

GIFT BOX

The charming gift box pattern is inspired by the excitement of gift-giving during the holiday season. Adorned with its big, beautiful ribbon, it reminds us of the magical moments spent unwrapping gifts with loved ones, each present holding a special memory or thoughtful gesture.

YARN

1 skein of each color for the box and ribbon.

Fingering weight (#1 super fine) yarn, shown in Hobbii *Friends Cotton 8/4* (100% cotton, 174 yd. / 160 m per 1.75 oz / 50 g skein).

You can use any color combination you want for the present box and the ribbon.

The colors I used were:

BOX

42 Cranberry

89 Deep Ocean

05 Beige

RIBBON

13 Ochre

28 Mustard

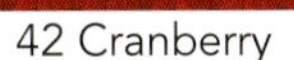

FINISHED MEASUREMENTS

HEIGHT: 1.6 in. / 4 cm

WIDTH: 1.6 in. / 4 cm

HOOK

- US B-1 / 2.25 mm crochet hook

NOTIONS

- Polyester stuffing (it is optional to stuff the present box)
- Tapestry needle
- Removable stitch markers
- Straight pins

GAUGE

Gauge is not critical for this project. Ensure your stitches are tight so the stuffing won't show through.

NOTE

To ensure that the crocheted piece will remain square, always make sure that your stitches are a bit tighter in the corners (the 3 sc together).

For more information on how to make the Box, including tips, step-by-step pictures, and videos, scan this QR code!

BOX

With the color of your choice, make a magic ring.
Rnd 1: 8 sc in ring
Rnd 2: 8 inc [16]
Rnd 3: (3 sc tog, 3 sc) x 4 [24]
Rnd 4: 1 sc, (3 sc tog, 5 sc) x 3, 3 sc tog, 4 sc [32]
Rnd 5: 2 sc, (3 sc tog, 7 sc) x 3, 3 sc tog, 5 sc [40]
Rnd 6: 3 sc, (3 sc tog, 9 sc) x 3, 3 sc tog, 6 sc [48]
Rnd 7: 4 sc, (3 sc tog, 11 sc) x 3, 3 sc tog, 7 sc [56]
Rnd 8: BPsc 56
Rnds 9–22: 56 sc (14 rounds)
Fasten off.

LID

With the color of your choice, make a magic ring.
Rnd 1: 8 sc in ring
Rnd 2: 8 inc [16]
Rnd 3: (3 sc tog, 3 sc) x 4 [24]
Rnd 4: 1 sc, (3 sc tog, 5 sc) x 3, 3 sc tog, 4 sc [32]
Rnd 5: 2 sc, (3 sc tog, 7 sc) x 3, 3 sc tog, 5 sc [40]
Rnd 6: 3 sc, (3 sc tog, 9 sc) x 3, 3 sc tog, 6 sc [48]
Rnd 7: 4 sc, (3 sc tog, 11 sc) x 3, 3 sc tog, 7 sc [56]
Rnd 8: 5 sc, (3 sc tog, 13 sc) x 3, 3 sc tog, 8 sc [64]
Rnd 9: BLO 64 sc
Rnds 10–12: 64 sc (3 rounds)
Rnd 13: FLO 64 sl st
Fasten off.

RIBBON

The Ribbon is made in 3 parts:

PART I

With the color of your choice, work 43 chains and from the second chain from the hook make:

Row 1: 1 sl st, 19 sc, 2 sl st, 19 sc, 1sl st, chain and turn

Rows 2–7: BLO 1 sl st, 19 sc, 2 sl st, 19 sc, 1sl st, chain and turn (6 rows)

Leave a long thread to sew. Sew both endings closing it into a circle.

PART 2

Start with 29 chains and for the second chain from the hook make:

Row 1: 13 sc, 2 sl st, 13 sc, chain and turn.

Rows 2–3: BLO 13 sc, 2 sl st, 13 sc, chain and turn (2 rows)

Fasten off.

PART 3

Start with 13 chains and for the second chain from the hook make:

Row 1: 12 sc, chain and turn

Row 2: 12 sc

Leave a long thread to sew.

Position Part 3 in the middle of Part I of the Ribbon. Sew both endings of Part 3 to close it and form a lace. Keep the remaining thread to sew the Ribbon to the Box.

Place Part 2 of the Ribbon inside the lace. Sew the Ribbon in the middle of the Lid of the Box and fasten off.

RESIDENTS *of* *the* NORTH POLE

Handmade
with love
Handmade
with love

SANTA CLAUS

Who better than Santa Claus to remind ourselves that it is already Christmas season? Creating Santa Claus was truly a labor of love, inspired by the warmth and joy of the holiday season. When I think of Christmas, Santa is one of the first images that comes to mind—jolly and generous, a symbol of giving and cheer. Whether you choose to create the full figure or just the head as an ornament to adorn your Christmas tree or wreath, this charming pattern is perfect to decorate your home with the holiday spirit.

YARN

1 skein of each of these colors:

Fingering weight (#1 super fine) yarn, shown in Scheepjes *Catona* (100% cotton,174 yd. / 125 m per 1.75 oz / 50 g skein)

SHIRT STRIPES

157 Root Beer

Fingering weight (#1 super fine) yarn, shown in Hobbii *Friends Cotton 8/4* (100% cotton, 174 yd. / 160 m per 1.75 oz / 50 g skein)

BOOTS

123 Charcoal

Fingering weight (#1 super fine) yarn, shown in Hobbii *Friends Cotton 8/4 Mercerized* (100% cotton, 174 yd. / 160 m per 1.75 oz / 50 g skein)

SKIN

04 Cream

OVERALLS/HAT

42 Cranberry

BEARD/MUSTACHE/HAT/SHIRT

01 White

Lace yarn (#0 lace), shown in Hobbii *Rainbow Lace* (100% cotton, 306 yd. / 280 m per 1.75 oz / 50 g ball)

EMBROIDERY

009 Black

Note: *Any standard black embroidery thread can be used.*

FINISHED MEASUREMENTS

WHOLE BODY HEIGHT: 5.5 in. / 14 cm
WIDTH: 2 in. / 5 cm
HEAD HEIGHT: 2.4 in. / 6 cm
HEAD WIDTH: 2.75 in. / 7 cm

HOOK

- US B-1 / 2.25 mm hook

NOTIONS

- Polyester stuffing
- Tapestry needle
- Removable stitch markers
- Straight pins
- Two buttons for Suspenders (optional)
- Amigurumi glasses or craft wire to create the glasses
- Pair of pointy tweezers
- Makeup blush (optional)
- Craft glue

GAUGE

Gauge is not critical for this project. Ensure your stitches are tight so the stuffing won't show through.

For more information on how to make Santa Claus, including tips, step-by-step pictures, and videos, scan this QR code!

HEAD

With **Cream**, make a magic ring.

Rnd 1: 8 sc in ring

Rnd 2: 8 inc [16]

Rnd 3: (1 sc, 1 inc) x 8 [24]

Rnd 4: 1 sc, 1 inc, (2 sc, 1 inc) x 7, 1 sc [32]

Rnd 5: (3 sc, 1 inc) x 8 [40]

Rnd 6: 2 sc, 1 inc, (4 sc, 1 inc) x 7, 2 sc [48]

Rnd 7: (5 sc, 1 inc) x 8 [56]

Rnds 8–17: 56 sc (10 rounds)

Rnd 18: 16 sc, (2 sc, 1 inc) x 8, 16 sc [64].

Rnds 19–21: 64 sc (3 rounds)

Rnd 22: 3 sc, 1 dec, (6 sc, 1 dec) x 7, 3 sc [56]

Rnd 23: (5 sc, 1 dec) x 8 [48]

Rnd 24: 2 sc, 1 dec, (4 sc, 1 dec) x 7, 2 sc [40]

Rnd 25: (3 sc, 1 dec) x 8 [32]

Rnd 26: 1 sc, 1 dec, (2 sc, 1 dec) x 7, 1 sc [24]

Rnd 27: (1 sc, 1 dec) x 8 [16]

Rnd 28: 8 dec [8]

Stuff the Head before finishing off with the inverted magic ring.

Mark the first and last increases in round 18 (before stitch 19 and after stitch 48) as they mark the front of the face–this is where we will place Santa's Ears, Nose, and Eyes.

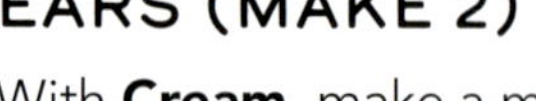

EARS (MAKE 2)

With **Cream**, make a magic ring.

Rnd 1: 7 hdc in ring

Finish off and leave a long thread to sew.

Attach the Ears to the Head at the place where you have the pins, between rounds 15 and 18.

NOSE

With **Cream**, make a magic ring.

Rnd 1: 6 sc in ring

Rnd 2: 6 inc [12]

Rnd 3: 12 sc

Fasten off and leave a long thread to sew. Stuff the Nose slightly and attach it to the Head between rounds 15 and 18 (same height as the Ears), right in the middle of the face. You should have about 8 sc between the Nose and each Ear.

Embroider the Eyes and Eyelashes following the instructions on page 132.

If you want to create rosy Cheeks, apply some blush to your Santa Claus's Cheek and Nose.

EYEBROWS (MAKE 2)

With **White**.

Make 6 chains and finish leaving a long thread.

Attach the Eyebrows between rounds 10 and 12, using 5 sc wide.

To finish off, pass both ends through the Head making them leave on the same gap. Then, tie a knot with them and push this knot inside the Head to hide it.

MUSTACHE (MAKE 2)

With **White**, make a magic ring.
Rnd 1: 6 sc in ring
Rnd 2: 6 sc
Rnd 3: 2 inc, 4 sc [8]
Rnd 4: 8 sc
Rnd 5: (1 sc, 1 inc) x 2, 4 sc [10]
Rnd 6: 10 sc
Rnd 7: (2 sc, 1 inc) x 2, 4 sc [12]
Rnds 8–9: 12 sc (2 rounds)
Rnd 10: 3 dec, 6 sc [9]
Rnd 11: 9 sc
Rnd 12: (1 sc, 1 dec) x 3 [6]
Don't stuff the Mustache. Fasten off both pieces.

BEARD

Santa's Beard is made in 3 layers to give volume and depth to this very important part of our character.

Layer 1

With **White**, work 28 chains and from the second chain make 27 sl st. Make 2 chains and 3 Tr in the same stitch. Make another chain and 2 sl st in the next stitches. Make 2 chains and repeat the sequence 9 times. Finish off.

Layer 2

Make 25 chains and from the second chain make 24 sl st. Make 1 chain and 3 Dc in the same stitch. Make another chain and 2 sl st in the next stitches. Make 1 chain and repeat the sequence 8 times.

Finish off.

Layer 3

Make 19 chains and from the second chain make 18 sl st. Make 1 chain and 3 hdc in the same stitch.

Make another chain and 2 sl st in the next stitches. Make 1 chain and repeat the sequence 6 times.

Finish off.

Position Layer 1 of the Beard from Santa Claus's Ear to Ear. Position Layer 2 of the Beard on top of Layer 1, and Layer 3 on top of Layer 2.

Glue the 3 Layers of the Beard. Then position the Mustaches just below the Nose and glue them in place.

I always advise positioning all the parts with pins before gluing, to make sure they are in the desired position.

LEFT LEG

With **Charcoal**.

We will work on both sides of the chains. Start with 5 chains and from the second chain from the hook make:

Rnd 1: 3 sc, in the last chain 3 sc, continue on the other side of the chains 2 sc, 1 inc [10]

Rnd 2: 1 inc, 2 sc, 3 inc, 2 sc, 2 inc [16]

Rnd 3: (1 sc, 1 inc), 2 sc, (1 sc, 1 inc) x 3, 2 sc, (1 sc, 1 inc) x 2 [22]

Rnd 4: BPsc 22

Rnds 5–6: 22 sc (2 rounds)

Rnd 7: 6 sc, (1 sc, 1 dec) x 3, 7 sc [19]

Rnd 8: 6 sc, 3 dec, 7 sc [16]

Rnd 9: 6 sc, 1 dec triple, 7 sc [14]

Rnd 10: FLO 14 sl st

Rnd 11: Change to **Cranberry**. BLO (6 sc, 1 inc) x 2 [16]

Rnd 12: (3 sc, 1 inc) x 4 [20]

Rnds 13–14: 20 sc (2 rounds)

Stuff the Leg and fasten off.

If you want your Santa to have flat Feet to stand, make sure that you don't stuff it too much and leave it concave.

RIGHT LEG AND BODY

Repeat rounds 1 to 14 of the Left Leg.

Make 2 more sc and 1 chain to get to the side of the Leg. Be sure that both Feet are facing forward at the junction of the Legs.

Rnd 15: 20 sc, 1 sc on the chain, 20 sc, 1 sc on the chain [42]

Rnd 16: 15 sc, (1 sc, 1 inc) x 6, 15 sc [48]

Rnd 17: 48 sc
Rnd 18: 15 sc, (2 sc, 1 inc) x 6, 15 sc [54]
Rnds 19–21: 54 sc (3 rounds)
Rnd 22: 15 sc, (2 sc, 1 dec) x 6, 15 sc [48]
Rnd 23: 48 sc
Rnd 24: (6 sc, 1 dec) x 6 [42]
Rnd 25: 42 sc
Rnd 26: (5 sc, 1 dec) x 6 [36]
Rnd 27: Change to **White**: BLO 36 sc
Rnd 28: 36 sc
Rnd 29: Change to **Root Beer**. 36 sc
Rnd 30: Change to **White**: (4 sc, 1 dec) x 6 [30]
Rnd 31: 30 sc
Rnd 32: Change to **Root Beer**: 30 sc
Rnd 33: Change to **White**: 30 sc
Rnd 34: 30 sc
Rnd 35: Change to **Root Beer**: 30 sc
Rnd 36: Change to **Cream**: BLO 30 sc
Stuff the Body and leave a long thread to sew.

SUSPENDERS

With **Cranberry**.
Insert the hook into the first loop formed by round 27. Make 4 sl st and 22 chains.
From the second chain from the hook, make 21 sc and close with 1 sl st in the next loop of round 27.
Make additional 28 sl st and 22 chains.
From the second chain from the hook, make 21 sc and close with 1 sl st in the next loop of round 27. Make more 3 sl st on round 27 and finish off.

ARMS (MAKE 2)

With **Cream**, make a magic ring.

Rnd 1: 6 sc in ring

Rnd 2: (1 sc, 1 inc) x 3 [9]

Rnd 3: 8 sc, 3 hdc in the same st [11]

Rnd 4: 8 sc, 1 dec triple [9]

Rnd 5: 9 sc

Rnd 6: Change to **Root Beer**: 9 sc

Rnd 7: Change to **White**: 9 sc

Rnd 8: 9 sc

Rnd 9: Change to **Root Beer**: 9 sc

Rnd 10: Change to **White**: 9 sc

Rnd 11: 9 sc

Rnd 12: Change to **Root Beer**: 9 sc

Rnd 13: Change to **White**: 9 sc

Rnd 14: 9 sc

Slightly stuff half of the Arms (until round 8) and leave a long thread to sew.

Pinch closed the Arm opening and sew it together with the remaining yarn.

Sew the Arms between rounds 34 and 35 with the Thumbs facing up (the Thumbs are the 3 hdc of round 3).

Adjust the Suspender straps by passing them over the Arms. Place buttons at the tips of the Suspender's straps and sew them with a red thread that fits your chosen buttons.

You can either sew on the Suspenders or use a button to attach it to the front.

GLASSES

There are several models of amigurumi Glasses on the market. You can choose to buy Glasses or make one using craft wire.

If you prefer to make your own Glasses, scan the QR code to watch the tutorial.

HAT

With **White**, make a magic ring.

Rnd 1: 6 sc in ring

Rnd 2: 6 inc [12]

Rnd 3: (1 sc, 1 inc) x 6 [18]

Rnds 4–6: 18 sc (3 rounds)

Rnd 7: (1 sc, 1 dec) x 6 [12]

Rnd 8: 6 dec [6]

Rnd 9: Change to **Cranberry**: 6 sc

Rnd 10: 6 inc [12]

Rnds 11–12: 12 sc (2 rounds)

Rnd 13: (1 sc, 1 inc) x 6 [18]

Rnds 14–16: 18 sc (3 rounds)

Rnd 17: (5 sc, 1 inc) x 3 [21]

Rnds 18–19: 21 sc (2 rounds)

Rnd 20: 3 sc, 1 inc, (6 sc, 1 inc) x 2, 3 sc [24]

Rnds 21–22: 24 sc (2 rounds)

Rnd 23: (3 sc, 1 inc) x 6 [30]

Rnd 24: 30 sc

Rnd 25: (4 sc, 1 inc) x 6 [36]

Rnd 26: 36 sc

Rnd 27: (5 sc, 1 inc) x 6 [42]

Rnd 28: 42 sc

Rnd 29: 3 sc, 1 inc, (6 sc, 1 inc) x 5, 3 sc [48]

Rnd 30: 48 sc

Rnd 31: (7 sc, 1 inc) x 6 [54]

Rnd 32: 54 sc

Rnd 33: 4 sc, 1 inc, (8 sc, 1 inc) x 5, 4 sc [60]

Rnd 34: 60 sc

Rnd 35: Change to **White**: BLO 60 sl st

Rnd 36: BLO 60 sc

Rnd 37: 60 hdc

Rnd 38: 60 sl st

Finish off.

To sew the Body to the Head, see the instructions on page 135.

MRS. CLAUS

With her kind heart and welcoming spirit, Mrs. Claus joins the holiday season to ensure that all preparations are full of joy and love. She is the perfect addition to charm our Christmas decor, and just like Santa Claus, you can crochet only her head for a sweet ornament on your Christmas tree or crochet the full figure to stand beside Santa.

YARN

1 skein of each of these colors:

Fingering weight (#1 super fine) yarn, shown in Scheepjes *Catona* (100% cotton, 174 yd. / 125 m per 1.75 oz / 50 g skein)

SHIRT STRIPES

157 Root Beer

Fingering weight (#1 super fine) yarn, shown in Hobbii *Friends Cotton 8/4 Mercerized* (100% cotton, 174 yd. / 160 m per 1.75 oz / 50 g skein)

SKIN

04 Cream

DRESS/SHIRT

01 White

DRESS/RIBBON

42 Cranberry

HAIR

117 Light Gray

Fingering weight (#1 super fine) yarn, shown in Hobbii *Friends Cotton 8/4* (100% cotton, 174 yd. / 160 m per 1.75 oz / 50g skein)

BOOTS

123 Charcoal

Fingering weight (#1 super fine) yarn, shown in Hobbii *Tencel Bamboo Fine* (40% Tencel, 60% bamboo viscose, 230 yd. / 210 m per 1.8 oz / 50 g skein)

EARRINGS

17473 Curry

Lace yarn (#0 lace), shown in Hobbii *Rainbow Lace* (100% cotton, 306 yd. / 280 m per 1.75 oz / 50 g ball)

EMBROIDERY

009 Black

Note: *Any standard black embroidery thread can be used.*

FINISHED MEASUREMENTS

WHOLE BODY HEIGHT: 5.5 in. / 14 cm
WIDTH: 2 in. / 5 cm
HEAD HEIGHT: 2.4 in. / 6 cm
HEAD WIDTH: 2.75 in. / 7 cm

HOOK

- US B-1 / 2.25 mm hook

NOTIONS

- Polyester stuffing
- Tapestry needle
- Removable stitch markers
- Straight pins
- Pair of pointy tweezers
- Makeup blush (optional)
- Craft glue

GAUGE

Gauge is not critical for this project. Ensure your stitches are tight so the stuffing won't show through.

SPECIAL STITCHES

- **FRENCH KNOT:** See instructions on page 132.

For more information on how to make Mrs. Claus, including tips, step-by-step pictures, and videos, scan this QR code!

HEAD

With **Cream**, make a magic ring.
Rnd 1: 8 sc in ring
Rnd 2: 8 inc [16]
Rnd 3: (1 sc, 1 inc) x 8 [24]
Rnd 4: 1 sc, 1 inc, (2 sc, 1 inc) x 7, 1 sc [32]
Rnd 5: (3 sc, 1 inc) x 8 [40]
Rnd 6: 2 sc, 1 inc, (4 sc, 1 inc) x 7, 2 sc [48]
Rnd 7: (5 sc, 1 inc) x 8 [56]
Rnds 8–17: 56 sc (10 rounds)
Rnd 18: 16 sc, (2 sc, 1 inc) x 8, 16 sc [64]
Rnds 19–21: 64 sc (3 rounds)
Rnd 22: 3 sc, 1 dec, (6 sc, 1 dec) x 7, 3 sc [56]
Rnd 23: (5 sc, 1 dec) x 8 [48]
Rnd 24: 2 sc, 1 dec, (4 sc, 1 dec) x 7, 2 sc [40]
Rnd 25: (3 sc, 1 dec) x 8 [32]
Rnd 26: 1 sc, 1 dec, (2 sc, 1 dec) x 7, 1 sc [24]
Rnd 27: (1 sc, 1 dec) x 8 [16]
Rnd 28: 8 dec [8]
Stuff the Head before finishing off with the inverted magic ring.
Mark the first and last increases in round 18 (before stitch 19 and after stitch 48) as they mark the front of the face–this is where we will place Mrs. Claus's Ears, Nose and Eyes.

EARS (MAKE 2)

With **Cream**, make a magic ring.
Rnd 1: 7 hdc in ring
Finish off and leave a long thread to sew.
Attach the Ears to the Head at the place where you have the pins, between rounds 15 and 18.

NOSE

With **Cream**, make a magic ring.
Rnd 1: 6 sc in ring
Rnd 2: 6 inc [12]
Rnd 3: 12 sc
Fasten off and leave a long thread to sew. Stuff the Nose slightly and attach it to the Head between rounds 15 and 18 (same height as the Ears), right in the middle of the face. You should have about 8 sc between the Nose and each Ear.
Embroider the Eyes and Eyelashes following the instructions on page 132. If you want to create rosy Cheeks, apply some blush to Mrs. Claus's Cheeks and Nose.

EYEBROWS (MAKE 2)

With **Light Gray**.
Make 6 chains and finish leaving a long thread.
Attach the Eyebrows between rounds 10 and 12, using 5 sc wide.
To finish off, pass both ends through the Head making them leave on the same gap. Then, tie a knot with them and push this knot inside the Head to hide it.

HAIR

With **Light Gray**, make a magic ring.

The hair is made in 2 parts.

PART 1 (HAIR)

Rnd 1: 8 sc in ring
Rnd 2: 8 inc [16]
Rnd 3: (1 sc, 1 inc) x 8 [24]
Rnd 4: 1 sc, 1 inc, (2 sc, 1 inc) x 7, 1 sc [32]
Rnd 5: (3 sc, 1 inc) x 8 [40]
Rnd 6: 2 sc, 1 inc, (4 sc, 1 inc) x 7, 2 sc [48]
Rnd 7: (5 sc, 1 inc) x 8 [56]
Rnds 8–12: 56 sc (5 rounds)
Make 28 sc and turn. From this round on, we will turn the piece without making chains to turn.
So that the "V" formed in Mrs. Claus's hair is perfect, let's turn the piece at the end of each round without making the chains. A very valuable tip is to keep the loop very tight on the hook, so that there is no gap where you skip the stitch.
Note: Instead of inserting the hook into the first sc, skip this stitch and insert it into the second sc.
Rnd 13: Skip 1 sc, 53 sc, skip 1 sc, 1 sc, turn [54]
Rnd 14: Skip 1 sc, 51 sc, skip 1 sc, 1 sc, turn [52]
Rnd 15: Skip 1 sc, 49 sc, skip 1 sc, 1 sc, turn [50]
Rnd 16: Skip 1 sc, 47 sc, skip 1 sc, 1 sc, turn [48]
Make sl st around all Hair to complete the finish and then fasten off.

PART 2 (BUN)

With **Light Gray**, make a magic ring.
Rnd 1: 6 sc in ring
Rnd 2: 6 inc [12]
Rnd 3: (1 sc, 1 inc) x 6 [18]
Rnd 4: 1 sc, 1 inc, (2 sc, 1 inc) x 5, 1 sc [24]
Rnd 5: (3 sc, 1 inc) x 6 [30]
Rnd 6: 2 sc, 1 inc, (4 sc, 1 inc) x 5, 2 sc [36]
Rnds 7–10: 36 sc (4 rounds)
Leave a long thread to sew.
Pin the Bun on top of the Hair and stuff it before sewing. You can choose to glue the Hair on the Head, or just place it without gluing.

ROMANIAN LACE

To make the Ribbon for the Hair, we will make the Romanian Lace cord with **Cranberry**. You will need two pieces: one to fasten around the Bun and another to assemble the Ribbon bow that we will glue on top.
You can learn this technique by watching the video with the QR Code, or by following this step-by-step:
Make a slip knot and 2 chains. From the second chain, make 1 sc.
Turn the piece clockwise and insert the hook into the two loops on the left to make 1 sc.
Repeat these 2 steps until it gets to the desired size (enough to wrap around the Bun and make the Ribbon Bow)
I always advise positioning all parts with pins before gluing, to make sure they are in the desired position.

EARRINGS

For the Earrings make two French Knots (see page 132) with **Curry**, one for each Ear.

LEFT LEG

With **Charcoal**.

We will work on both sides of the chains. Start with 5 chains and from the second chain from the hook, make:

Rnd 1: 3 sc, in the last chain 3 sc, continue on the other side of the chain 2 sc, 1 inc [10]

Rnd 2: 1 inc, 2 sc, 3 inc, 2 sc, 2 inc [16]

Rnd 3: (1 sc, 1 inc), 2 sc, (1 sc, 1 inc) x 3, 2 sc, (1 sc, 1 inc) x 2 [22]

Rnd 4: BPsc 22

Rnds 5–6: 22 sc (2 rounds)

Rnd 7: 6 sc, (1 sc, 1 dec) x 3, 7 sc [19]

Rnd 8: 6 sc, 3 dec, 7 sc [16]

Rnd 9: 6 sc, 1 dec triple, 7 sc [14]

Rnd 10: FLO 14 sl st

Fasten off.

Insert the hook in the back loops from round 10, to continue the Legs.

Rnd 11: Change to **White**. BLO (6 sc, 1 inc) x 2 [16]

Rnd 12: (3 sc, 1 inc) x 4 [20]

Rnd 13: Change to **Root Beer**. 20 sc

Rnd 14: Change to **White**. 20 sc

Stuff the Leg and fasten off.

If you want Mrs. Claus to have flat Feet to stand, make sure that you don't stuff it too much and leave it concave.

RIGHT LEG AND BODY

Repeat rounds 1 to 14 of the Left Leg.

Make 2 more sc and 1 chain to get to the side of the Leg. Be sure that both Feet are facing forward at the junction of the Legs.

Rnd 15: 20 sc on the Left Leg, 1 sl st at the same stitch where the round started,

20 sc on the Right Leg [41]

Rnd 16: Change to **Root Beer**. 20 sc on the Left Leg, skip 1 sl st, 20 sc on the Right Leg [40]

Rnd 17: Change to **White**. 40 sc

Rnd 18–20: 40 sc (3 rounds)

Rnd 21: (6 sc, 1 dec) x 5 [35]

Rnd 22: 35 sc

Rnd 23: Change to **Cranberry**. 35 sc

Rnd 24: 35 sc

Rnd 25: BLO 35 sc

Rnd 26: 35 sc

Rnd 27: (5 sc, 1 dec) x 7 [30]

Rnds 28–31: 30 sc (4 rounds)

Rnd 32: Change to **Cream**. BLO 30 sc.

Rnd 33: (3 sc, 1 dec) x 6 [24]

Stuff the Body and leave a long thread to sew.

SKIRT

With **Cranberry**, insert the hook into the loops formed by round 25 of the Body.

Rnd 1: (4 sc, 1 inc) x 7 [42]

Rnd 2: (2 sc, 1 inc) x 14 [56]

Rnds 3–7: 56 sc (5 rounds)

Rnd 8: FLO 56 sc–Finish off.

Insert the hook into the back loops formed by round 8 of the Skirt.

Change to **White**.

Rnd 9: (1 sc, 1 hdc, 1 dc, 1 chain 1 sl st) x 14
Fasten off.

COLLAR

With **White**.
To make the collar we will use the loops formed by round 32 of the Body. Position the Body upside down and insert the hook in the first loop.
Rnd 1: 30 sl st
Rnd 2: BLO (11 sc, 2 hdc, 1 chain, 1 inc Dc, 1 chain, 1 sl st, 1 chain, 1 inc Dc, 1 chain, 2 hdc, 12 sc).
Fasten off.

ARMS (MAKE 2)

With **Cream**, make a magic ring.
Rnd 1: 6 sc in ring
Rnd 2: (1 sc, 1 inc) x 3 [9]
Rnd 3: 8 sc, 3 hdc in the same stitch [11]
Rnd 4: 8 sc, 1 dec triple [9]
Rnd 5: 9 sc
Rnd 6: Change to **Root Beer**: 9 sc
Rnd 7: Change to **White**: 9 sc
Rnd 8: 9 sc
Rnd 9: Change to **Root Beer**: 9 sc
Rnd 10: Change to **White**: 9 sc
Rnd 11: Change to **Cranberry**. FLO 9 inc [18]
Rnd 12: 18 sc
Rnd 13: 18 sc
Rnd 14: 9 dec [9]
Slightly stuff half of the Arms (until round 8) and leave a long thread to sew.
Pinch closed the Arm opening and sew it together with the remaining yarn.

Sew the Arms between rounds 30 and 31 with the Thumbs facing up (the Thumbs are the 3 hdc of round 3).

To sew the Body to the Head, see the instructions on page 135.

Handmade
with love

HOLLY THE ELF

Elves have always been a beloved part of Christmas, known for their playful spirit and tireless work helping Santa prepare gifts. Holly and Jolly, with their ginger hair, freckles, and the red and green outfits, capture this spirit perfectly.

YARN

1 skein of each of these colors:

Fingering weight (#1 super fine) yarn, shown in Hobbii *Friends Cotton 8/4 Mercerized* (100% cotton, 174 yd. / 160 m per 1.75 oz / 50 g skein)

SKIN

04 Cream

BOOTS

12 Chocolate

OUTFIT/HAT

01 White

112 Bottle Green

DRESS/HAT

42 Cranberry

HAIR

17 Cognac

Lace yarn (#0 lace), shown in Hobbii *Rainbow Lace* (100% cotton, 306 yd. / 280 m per 1.75 oz / 50 g ball)

EMBROIDERY

006 Light Brown

Fingering weight (#1 super fine) yarn, Hobbii Tencel Bamboo Fine (40% Tencel, 60% bamboo viscose, 230 yd. / 210 m per 1.8 oz / 50 g skein)

SKIRT DETAIL

17473 Curry

FINISHED MEASUREMENTS

WHOLE BODY HEIGHT: 5.5 in. / 14 cm
WIDTH: 1.5 in. / 4 cm
HEAD HEIGHT: 2.4 in. / 6 cm
HEAD WIDTH: 3.55 in. / 9 cm

HOOK

- US B-1 / 2.25 mm hook for the Body, Hat, and Outfit
- US C-2 / 2.50 mm hook for the Hair

NOTIONS

- Polyester stuffing
- Tapestry needle
- Removable stitch markers
- Straight pins
- Craft glue
- Makeup blush (optional)
- Pair of pointy tweezers
- Pair of 12 mm safety eyes

GAUGE

Gauge is not critical for this project. Ensure your stitches are tight so the stuffing won't show through.

For more information on how to make Holly, including tips, step-by-step pictures, and videos, scan this QR code!

HEAD

With smaller hook and **Cream**, make a magic ring.
Rnd 1: 8 sc in ring
Rnd 2: 8 inc [16]
Rnd 3: (1 sc, 1 inc) x 8 [24]
Rnd 4: 1 sc, 1 inc, (2 sc, 1 inc) x 7, 1 sc [32]
Rnd 5: (3 sc, 1 inc) x 8 [40]
Rnd 6: 2 sc, 1 inc, (4 sc, 1 inc) x 7, 2 sc [48]
Rnd 7: (5 sc, 1 inc) x 8 [56]
Rnds 8–17: 56 sc (10 rounds)
Rnd 18: (3 sc, 1 inc) x 14 [70]
Insert the Eyes between rounds 16 and 17 with 7 sc of visible distance.
Rnds 19–21: 70 sc (3 rounds)
Rnd 22: (3 sc, 1 dec) x 14 [56]
Rnd 23: 56 sc
Rnd 24: 1 sc, 1 dec, (2 sc, 1 dec) x 13, 1 sc [42]
Rnd 25: (5 sc, 1 dec) x 6 [36]
Rnd 26: 2 sc, 1 dec, (4 sc, 1 dec) x 5, 2 sc [30]
Rnd 27: (3 sc, 1 dec) x 6 [24]
Rnd 28: 1 sc, 1 dec, (2 sc, 1 dec) x 5, 1 sc [18]
Rnd 29: (1 sc, 1 dec) x 6 [12]
Rnd 30: 6 dec [6]
Stuff the Head before finishing off with the inverted magic ring.
Make the Nose between rounds 17 and 18, 2 sc away from the Eyes, using the space of 3 sc.
With **Light Brown** embroider the Eyebrows between rounds 11 and 12, using the space of 4 sc.
With **Light Brown** embroider the Eyelashes.
With **White** embroider the eye contour on the outer corner of the Eyes.
With **Cognac**, make the freckles on the doll's face, always using the space of 1 sc. Make these stitches just below the Eyes, so that they are:
1 stitch between rounds 19 and 20.
3 stitches between rounds 20 and 21.
1 stitch between rounds 21 and 22.
You can space them however you feel is more harmonic, and even make more or less freckles.

EARS (MAKE 2)

With smaller hook and **Cream**, make a magic ring.
Rnd 1: 6 sc in ring
Rnd 2: (1 sc, 1 inc) x 3 [9]
Rnd 3: 9 sc
Rnd 4: (2 sc, 1 inc) x 3 [12]
Rnds 5–6: 12 sc (2 rounds)
Do not stuff the Ears. Pinch closed the Ears opening and make 6 sc to close it.
Leave a long thread to sew.
Sew the Ears between rounds 16 and 18, 3 sc away from the Eyes.

HAIR

With larger hook and **Cognac**, make a magic ring.

Rnd 1: 8 sc in ring

Rnd 2: 8 inc [16]

Rnd 3: (1 sc, 1 inc) x 8 [24]

Rnd 4: 1 sc, 1 inc, (2 sc, 1 inc) x 7, 1 sc [32]

Now we will work around the 32 sc of round 4 to make the Hair strands.

Sts 1–9: 22 chains, and from the second chain make 21 Hdc, sc in the next st.

St 10: 9 chains, and from the second chain make 8 Hdc, sc in the next st.

St 11: 1 sc

St 12: 11 chains, and from the second chain make 10 Hdc, sc in the next st.

St 13: 1 sc

St 14: 13 chains, and from the second chain make 12 Hdc, sc in the next st.

St 15: 1 sc

St 16: 15 chains, and from the second chain make 14 Hdc, sc in the next st.

St 17: 1 sc

St 18: 21 chains, and from the second chain make 20 Hdc, sc in the next st.

St 19: 1 sc

St 20: 13 chains, and from the second chain make 12 Hdc, sc in the next st.

St 21: 1 sc

St 22: 11 chains, and from the second chain make 10 Hdc, sc in the next st.

St 23: 9 chains, and from the second chain make 8 Hdc, sc in the next st.

Sts 24–31: 22 chains, and from the second chain make 21 Hdc, sc in the next st.

Note that the marker is behind the Head. The reverse side of the magic ring should stay up.

The strands 1 to 9 and 24 to 32 are behind the Ears. Strands 10 and 23 are above the Ears. Strands 12 to 18 are on the right side and strands 20 and 22 are on the left side.

LEFT LEG

With smaller hook and **Chocolate**.

We will work on both sides of the chains. Start with 5 chains and from the second chain make:

Rnd 1: 3 sc, in the last chain 3 sc, continue on the other side of the chain 2 sc, 1 inc [10]

Rnd 2: 1 inc, 2 sc, 3 inc, 2 sc, 2 inc [16]

Rnd 3: (1 sc, 1 inc), 2 sc, (1 sc, 1 inc) x 3, 2 sc, (1 sc, 1 inc) x 2 [22]

Rnd 4: BPsc 22

Rnds 5–6: 22 sc (2 rounds)

Rnd 7: 6 sc, (1 sc, 1 dec) x 3, 7 sc [19]

Rnd 8: 6 sc, 3 dec, 7 sc [16]

Rnd 9: 6 sc, 1 dec triple, 7 sc [14]

Rnd 10: 14 sc

Rnd 11: FLO 14 sl st

Rnd 12: Change to **White**. BLO (5 sc, 1 dec) x 2 [12]

Rnd 13: 12 sc

Rnd 14: Change to **Bottle Green**. 12 sc

Rnds 15–16: Change to **White**. 12 sc (2 rounds)

Rnd 17: 12 sc

Rnds 18–19: 12 sc (2 rounds)

Rnd 20: 12 sc

Stuff the Leg and fasten off.

If you want your Elf to have flat Feet to stand, make sure that you don't stuff them too much and leave them concave.

RIGHT LEG AND BODY

Repeat rounds 1 to 20 of the Left Leg. With the Right Leg, make more 3 sc to reach the side of the Leg using White.

Be sure that both Feet are facing forward at the junction of the Legs.

Make 2 chains and fasten them with 1 sc on the Left Leg. This will be the first stitch of the round.

Rnd 21: 12 sc, 2 sc in the chain, 12 sc, 2 sc in the chains [28]

Rnds 22–27: 28 sc (6 rounds)

Rnd 28: BLO 28 sc

Rnd 29: 28 sc

Rnds 30–31: 28 sc (2 rounds)

Rnd 32: 28 sc

Rnd 33: 28 sc

Rnd 34: (5 sc, 1 dec) x 4 [24]

Rnd 35: Change to **Cream**, BLO (4 sc, 1 dec) x 4 [20]

Stuff the Body and leave a long thread to sew.

ARMS (MAKE 2)

With larger hook and **Cream**, make a magic ring.

Rnd 1: 6 sc in ring

Rnd 2: (1 sc, 1 inc) x 3 [9]

Rnd 3: 8 sc, 3 Hdc in the same st [11]

Rnd 4: 8 sc, 1 dec triple [9]

Rnd 5: 9 sc

Rnd 6: Change to **Green**: 9 sc

Rnd 7: Change to **White**: 9 sc

Rnd 8: 9 sc

Rnd 9: Change to **Green**: 9 sc

Rnd 10: Change to **White**: 9 sc

Rnd 11: 9 sc

Rnd 12: Change to **Green**: 9 sc

Rnd 13: Change to **White**: 9 sc

Rnd 14: 9 sc

Slightly stuff half of the Arms (until round 8) and leave a long thread to sew.

Pinch closed the Arm opening and sew it together with the remaining yarn.

Sew the Arms between rounds 33 and 34 with the thumb of the hands facing upward (the thumbs are the 3 Hdc of round 3).

Adjust the strap of the Skirt Suspender by running it over one Arm.

SKIRT

With smaller hook and **Cranberry**.

Insert the hook in the first loop from round 28.

Rnd 1: 28 sl st

Rnd 2: BLO (3 sc, 1 inc) x 7 [35]

Rnd 3: 2 sc, 1 inc, (4 sc, 1 inc) x 6, 2 sc [42]

Rnd 4: 42 sc

Rnd 5: (5 sc, 1 inc) x 7 [49]

Rnds 6–7: 49 sc (2 rounds)

Rnd 8: Change to **Curry** and make 49 crab stitches. Finish off.

Insert the hook in the first loop of round 2. Make 18 sl st and 21 chains. Close it with 1 sl st in the last loop of round 2. Keep making sl st in the opposite direction in round 2 (10 sl st), until you reach the base of the Suspender strap. Fasten off.

HAT

With smaller hook and **White**, make a magic ring.

Rnd 1: 6 sc in ring

Rnd 2: 6 inc [12]

Rnd 3: (1 sc, 1 inc) x 6 [18]

Rnds 4–6: 18 sc (3 rounds)

Rnd 7: (1 sc, 1 dec) x 6 [12]

Rnd 8: 6 dec [6]

Rnd 9: Change to **Cranberry**. 6 Hdc

Rnd 10: Change to **Bottle Green**. (1 Hdc, 1 inc Hdc) x 3 [9]

Rnd 11: Change to **Cranberry**. 9 Hdc

Rnd 12: Change to **Bottle Green**. (2 Hdc, 1 inc Hdc) x 3 [12]

Rnd 13: Change to **Cranberry**. 12 Hdc

Rnd 14: Change to **Bottle Green**. 12 Hdc

Rnd 15: Change to **Cranberry**. 12 Hdc

Rnd 16: Change to **Bottle Green**. 12 Hdc

Rnd 17: Change to **Cranberry**. 12 Hdc

Rnd 18: Change to **Bottle Green**. (1 Hdc, 1 inc Hdc) x 6 [18]

Rnd 19: Change to **Cranberry**. 18 Hdc

Rnd 20: Change to **Bottle Green**. 1 Hdc, 1 inc Hdc, (2 Hdc, 1 inc Hdc) x 5, 1 Hdc [24]

Rnd 21: Change to **Cranberry**. 24 Hdc

Rnd 22: Change to **Bottle Green**. (2 Hdc, 1 inc Hdc) x 8 [32]

Rnd 23: Change to **Cranberry**. 32 Hdc

Rnd 24: Change to **Bottle Green**. (3 Hdc, 1 inc Hdc) x 8 [40]

Rnd 25: Change to **Cranberry**. 40 Hdc

Rnd 26: Change to **Bottle Green**. (2 Hdc, 1 inc Hdc), (4 Hdc, 1 inc Hdc) x 7, 2 Hdc [48]

Rnd 27: Change to **Cranberry**. 48 Hdc

Rnd 28: Change to **Bottle Green**. (5 Hdc, 1 inc Hdc) x 8 [56]

Rnd 29: Change to **Cranberry**. 3 Hdc, 1 inc Hdc, (6 Hdc, 1 inc Hdc) x 7, 3 Hdc [64]

Rnd 30: Change to **Bottle Green**. 64 Hdc

Rnds 31–32: Change to **White**: 64 Hdc (2 rounds)

Finish off.

If you want to create rosy Cheeks, apply some blush to your Elf's Cheeks and Nose. To sew the Body to the Head, see the instructions on page 135.

JOLLY THE ELF

Just like his friend Holly, Jolly is one of Santa's best helpers at the North Pole. His red-and-white-striped shirt and stockings are a nod to his favorite treat—candy canes!

YARN

1 skein of each of these colors:

Fingering weight (#1 super fine) yarn, shown in Hobbii Friends Cotton 8/4 Mercerized (100% cotton, 174 yd. / 160 m per 1.75 oz / 50 g skein)

SKIN

04 Cream

BOOTS

12 Chocolate

OUTFIT/HAT

01 White

SHORTS/HAT

42 Cranberry

SHORTS/HAT

112 Bottle Green

HAIR

17 Cognac

Lace yarn (#0 lace), shown in Hobbii *Rainbow Lace* (100% cotton, 306 yd. / 280 m per 1.75 oz / 50 g ball)

EMBROIDERY

006 Light Brown

FINISHED MEASUREMENTS

WHOLE BODY HEIGHT: 6.10 in. / 15.5 cm
WIDTH: 1.5 in. / 4 cm
HEAD HEIGHT: 2.75 in. / 7 cm
HEAD WIDTH: 3.55 in. / 9 cm

HOOK

- US B-1 / 2.25 mm hook for the Body, Hat, and Outfit
- US C-2 / 2.5 mm hook for the Hair

NOTIONS

- Polyester stuffing
- Tapestry needle
- Removable stitch markers
- Straight pins
- Craft glue
- Makeup blush (optional)
- Pair of pointy tweezers
- Pair of 12 mm safety eyes

GAUGE

Gauge is not critical for this project. Ensure your stitches are tight so the stuffing won't show through.

For more information on how to make Jolly, including tips, step-by-step pictures, and videos, scan this QR code!

HEAD

With **Cream** and smaller hook, make a magic ring.

Rnd 1: 8 sc in ring

Rnd 2: 8 inc [16]

Rnd 3: (1 sc, 1 inc) x 8 [24]

Rnd 4: 1 sc, 1 inc, (2 sc, 1 inc) x 7, 1 sc [32]

Rnd 5: (3 sc, 1 inc) x 8 [40]

Rnd 6: 2 sc, 1 inc, (4 sc, 1 inc) x 7, 2 sc [48]

Rnd 7: (5 sc, 1 inc) x 8 [56]

Rnds 8–17: 56 sc (10 rounds)

Rnd 18: (3 sc, 1 inc) x 14 [70]

Insert the Eyes between **rounds 16 and 17** with **7 sc** of visible distance.

Rnds 19–21: 70 sc (3 rounds)

Rnd 22: (3 sc, 1 dec) x 14 [56]

Rnd 23: 56 sc

Rnd 24: 1 sc, 1 dec, (2 sc, 1 dec) x 13, 1 sc [42]

Rnd 25: (5 sc, 1 dec) x 6 [36]

Rnd 26: 2 sc, 1 dec, (4 sc, 1 dec) x 5, 2 sc [30]

Rnd 27: (3 sc, 1 dec) x 6 [24]

Rnd 28: 1 sc, 1 dec, (2 sc, 1 dec) x 5, 1 sc [18]

Rnd 29: (1 sc, 1 dec) x 6 [12]

Rnd 30: 6 dec [6]

Stuff the Head before finishing off with the inverted magic ring.

Make the Nose between rounds 17 and 18, **2 sc** away from the Eyes, using the space of **3 sc**.

With **Light Brown** embroider the Eyebrows in rounds **11 and 12**, using the space of **4 sc**.

With **Light Brown** embroider the Eyelashes.

With **White** embroider the eye contour on the outer corner of the Eyes.

With **Cognac**, make the freckles on the doll's face, always using the space of **1 sc**. Make these stitches just above the Nose, so that they are:

1 stitch between **rounds 14 and 15**.

2 stitches between **rounds 15 and 16**.

3 stitches between **rounds 16 and 17**.

You can space them however you feel is more harmonic, and even make more or less freckles.

EARS (MAKE 2)

With **Cream** and smaller hook, make a magic ring.

Rnd 1: 6 sc in ring

Rnd 2: (1 sc, 1 inc) x 3 [9]

Rnd 3: 9 sc

Rnd 4: (2 sc, 1 inc) x 3 [12]

Rnds 5–6: 12 sc (2 rounds)

Do not stuff the Ears. Pinch closed the Ears opening and make 6 sc to close it.

Leave a long thread to sew.

Sew the Ears between rounds 16 and 18, 3 sc away from the Eyes.

SHORTS

With **Bottle Green** and smaller hook.

Make 18 chains and close it with 1 sc. This is the first st of the round.

Rnds 1–2: 18 sc (2 rounds)

Fasten off the first piece and make another one from round 1 to 2. Do not fasten off the second piece. With the second piece make 2 chains and join the first piece with 1 sc. This is the first st of the round from now on.

Rnd 3: 18 sc, 2 sc in the chains, 18 sc, 2 sc in the chains [40]

Rnds 4–6: 40 sc (3 rounds)

Rnd 7: 3 sc, 1 dec, (6 sc, 1 dec) x 4, 3 sc [35]

Rnd 8: 35 sc

Rnd 9: (3 sc, 1 dec) x 7 [28]

Leave the yarn attached to the Shorts. We will continue crocheting the Shorts later.

LEFT LEG

With **Chocolate** and smaller hook.

We will work on both sides of the chains. Start with 5 chains and from the second chain from the hook make:

Rnd 1: 3 sc, in the last chain 3 sc, continue on the other side of the chain 2 sc, 1 inc [10]

Rnd 2: 1 inc, 2 sc, 3 inc, 2 sc, 2 inc [16]
Rnd 3: (1 sc, 1 inc), 2 sc, (1 sc, 1 inc) x 3, 2 sc, (1 sc, 1 inc) x 2 [22]
Rnd 4: BPsc 22
Rnds 5–6: 22 sc (2 rounds)
Rnd 7: 6 sc, (1 sc, 1 dec) x 3, 7 sc [19]
Rnd 8: 6 sc, 3 dec, 7 sc [16]
Rnd 9: 6 sc, 1 dec triple, 7 sc [14]
Rnd 10: 14 sc
Rnd 11: FLO 14 sl st
Rnd 12: Change to **White**. BLO (5 sc, 1 dec) x 2 [12]
Rnd 13: 12 sc
Rnd 14: Change to **Cranberry**. 12 sc
Rnds 15–16: Change to **White**. 12 sc (2 rounds)
Rnd 17: 12 sc
Rnds 18–19: 12 sc (2 rounds)
Rnd 20: 12 sc
Stuff the Leg and fasten off.
If you want your Elf to have flat Feet to stand, make sure that you don't stuff it too much and leave it concave.

RIGHT LEG AND BODY

Repeat rounds 1 to 20 of the Left Leg. With the Right Leg, make more **3 sc** to reach the side of the Leg.
Place the Shorts on the Elf and leave them resting over the Feet, for we will continue crocheting just the Body. The Shorts will be crocheted with the Body further on!
To join the Legs, first make **2 chains** with the Right Leg and attach them with **1 sc** on the Left Leg. This will be the **first stitch** of the round.
Be sure that both Feet are facing forward at the junction of the Legs.
Rnd 21: 12 sc, 2 sc in the chain, 12 sc, 2 sc in the chains [28]
Rnds 22–27: 28 sc (6 rounds)–Fasten off!
Now we will join the Shorts to the Body!

Crochet both the Shorts and the Body together with **Bottle Green**. Make 28 sc joining both parts. This is round 28 of the Body!

Rnd 29: Change to **White**. BLO 28 sc
Rnd 30: 28 sc
Rnd 31: Change to **Cranberry**. 28 sc
Rnd 32: Change to **White**. 28 sc
Rnd 33: 28 sc
Rnd 34: Change to **Cranberry**. 28 sc
Rnd 35: Change to **White**. (5 sc, 1 dec) x 4 [24]
Rnd 36: Change to **Cream**. BLO 24 sc

Stuff the Body as you crochet and leave a long thread to sew it to the Head.

Insert the crochet hook in the loops from round 29. With **Bottle Green**, make 28 sl st and fasten off.

HAIR

With **Cognac** and larger hook, make a magic ring.

Rnd 1: 8 sc in ring
Rnd 2: 8 inc [16]
Rnd 3: BLO (1 sc, 1 inc) x 8 [24]
Rnd 4: 1 sc, 1 inc, (2 sc, 1 inc) x 7, 1 sc [32]
Rnd 5: BLO (3 sc, 1 inc) x 8 [40]
Rnd 6: 2 sc, 1 inc, (4 sc, 1 inc) x 7, 2 sc [48]
Rnd 7: BLO (5 sc, 1 inc) x 8 [56]
Rnd 8: 56 sc
Rnd 9: BLO 56 sc
Rnd 10: 56 sc
Rnd 11: BLO 56 sc
Rnd 12: 56 sc

Finish off.

CURLS

To make the Curls, we will work around the loops formed in the Hair, from the center to the edge of the piece. Make this sequence in a spiral until you finish all the loops of the Hair, including the front loops of round 12.

With **Cognac** and larger hook.

1 sc, 5 chains, 4 inc from the second chain from the hook.

2 sl st in the following loops.

HAT

With **White** and smaller hook, make a magic ring.

Rnd 1: 6 sc in ring
Rnd 2: 6 inc [12]
Rnd 3: (1 sc, 1 inc) x 6 [18]
Rnds 4–6: 18 sc (3 rounds)
Rnd 7: (1 sc, 1 dec) x 6 [12]
Rnd 8: 6 dec [6]
Rnd 9: Change to **Cranberry**. 6 Hdc
Rnd 10: Change to **Bottle Green**. (1 Hdc, 1 inc Hdc) x 3 [9]
Rnd 11: Change to **Cranberry**. 9 Hdc
Rnd 12: Change to **Bottle Green**. (2 Hdc, 1 inc Hdc) x 3 [12]
Rnd 13: Change to **Cranberry**. 12 Hdc
Rnd 14: Change to **Bottle Green**. 12 Hdc
Rnd 15: Change to **Cranberry**. 12 Hdc
Rnd 16: Change to **Bottle Green**. 12 Hdc
Rnd 17: Change to **Cranberry**. 12 Hdc
Rnd 18: Change to **Bottle Green**. (1 Hdc, 1 inc Hdc) x 6 [18]
Rnd 19: Change to **Cranberry**. 18 Hdc
Rnd 20: Change to **Bottle Green**. 1 Hdc, 1 inc Hdc, (2 Hdc, 1 inc Hdc) x 5, 1 Hdc [24]
Rnd 21: Change to **Cranberry**. 24 Hdc
Rnd 22: Change to **Bottle Green**. (2 Hdc, 1 inc Hdc) x 8 [32]
Rnd 23: Change to **Cranberry**. 32 Hdc
Rnd 24: Change to **Bottle Green**. (3 Hdc, 1 inc Hdc) x 8 [40]
Rnd 25: Change to **Cranberry**. 40 Hdc
Rnd 26: Change to **Bottle Green**. (2 Hdc, 1 inc Hdc, (4 Hdc, 1 inc Hdc) x 7, 2 Hdc [48]
Rnd 27: Change to **Cranberry**. 48 Hdc
Rnd 28: Change to **Bottle Green**. (5 Hdc, 1 inc Hdc) x 8 [56]
Rnd 29: Change to **Cranberry**. 3 Hdc, 1 inc Hdc, (6 Hdc, 1 inc Hdc) x 7, 3 Hdc [64]
Rnd 30: Change to **Bottle Green**. 64 Hdc
Rnds 31–32: Change to **White**: 64 Hdc. (2 rounds)

Finish off.

If you want to create rosy Cheeks, apply some blush to your Elf's Cheeks and Nose. To sew the Body to the Head of your Elf (see the instructions on page 135).

ARMS (MAKE 2)

With **Cream** and smaller hook, make a magic ring.

Rnd 1: 6 sc in magic ring.

Rnd 2: (1 sc, 1 inc) x 3 [9]

Rnd 3: 8 sc, 3 Hdc in the same st [11]

Rnd 4: 8 sc, 1 dec triple [9]

Rnd 5: 9 sc

Rnd 6: Change to **Cranberry**: 9 sc

Rnd 7: Change to **White**: 9 sc

Rnd 8: 9 sc

Rnd 9: Change to **Cranberry**: 9 sc

Rnd 10: Change to **White**: 9 sc

Rnd 11: 9 sc

Rnd 12: Change to **Cranberry**: 9 sc

Rnd 13: Change to **White**: 9 sc

Rnd 14: 9 sc

Slightly stuff half of the Arms (until round 8) and leave a long thread to sew.

Pinch closed the Arm opening and sew it together with the remaining yarn.

Sew the Arms between **rounds 35 and 36** with the thumb of the hands facing upward (the thumbs are the **3 Hdc** of **round 3**).

JASPER THE REINDEER

Among the most popular residents of the North Pole, Reindeer have always been a beloved part of Christmas, known for their role in guiding Santa's sleigh through the night sky to deliver presents to children around the world. With bright eyes, festive antlers, and warm mittens and socks, Jasper captures the tender and magical spirit of the story.

YARN

1 skein of each of these colors:

Fingering weight (#1 super fine) yarn, shown in Hobbii *Friends Cotton 8/4 Mercerized* (100% cotton, 174 yd. / 160 m per 1.75 oz / 50 g skein)

ANTLERS

12 Chocolate

SOCKS/MITTENS/SCARF

112 Bottle Green

Fingering weight (#1 super fine), shown in Hobbii *Bohème Velvet Fine* (100% polyester, 208 yd. / 190 m per 1.75 oz / 50 g skein)

SOCKS/MITTENS DETAILS

17616
Peridot Green

Fingering weight (#1 super fine) yarn, shown in Scheepjes *Catona* (100% mercerized cotton), 174 yd. / 125 m per 1.75 oz / 50 g skein)

SKIN TONE 1

157 Root Beer

SKIN TONE 2

105 Bridal White

FINISHED MEASUREMENTS

WHOLE BODY HEIGHT: 5.5 in. / 14 cm
WIDTH: 3.15 in. / 8 cm
HEAD HEIGHT: 2.4 in. / 6 cm
HEAD WIDTH: 4 in. / 10 cm

HOOK

- US B-1 / 2.25 mm hook

NOTIONS

- Polyester stuffing
- Tapestry needle
- Removable stitch markers
- Straight pins
- Pair of 12 mm safety eyes
- One 10 mm muzzle

GAUGE

Gauge is not critical for this project. Ensure your stitches are tight so the stuffing won't show through.

For more information on how to make Jasper, including tips, step-by-step pictures, and videos, scan this QR code!

HEAD

With **Root Beer**, make a magic ring.
Rnd 1: 8 sc in ring
Rnd 2: 8 inc [16]
Rnd 3: (1 sc, 1 inc) x 8 [24]
Rnd 4: 1 sc, 1 inc, (2 sc, 1 inc) x 7, 1 sc [32]
Rnd 5: (3 sc, 1 inc) x 8 [40]
Rnd 6: 2 sc, 1 inc, (4 sc, 1 inc) x 7, 2 sc [48]
Rnd 7: (5 sc, 1 inc) x 8 [56]
Rnds 8–13: 56 sc (6 rounds)
From rounds 14 to 18 we will make the many color changes. The color you work with is indicated before each part.
Rnd 14: (**Root Beer**) 19 sc, (**Bridal White**) 6 sc, (**Root Beer**) 6 sc, (**Bridal White**) 6 sc, (**Chestnut**) 19 sc [56]
Rnd 15: (**Root Beer**) 18 sc, (**Bridal White**) 8 sc, (**Root Beer**) 4 sc, (**Bridal White**) 8 sc, (**Chestnut**) 18 sc [56]
Rnds 16–17: (**Root Beer**) 17 sc, (**Bridal White**) 9 sc, (**Root Beer**) 4 sc, (**Bridal White**) 9 sc, (**Chestnut**) 17 sc [56]
Rnd 18: (**Root Beer**) (3 sc, 1 inc) x 4, (**Bridal White**) (3 sc, 1 inc) x 2, 2 sc, (**Root Beer**) 1 sc, 1 inc, 2 sc, (**Bridal White**) 1 sc, 1 inc, (3 sc, 1 inc) x 2, (**Root Beer**) (3 sc, 1 inc) x 4 [70]
Rnd 19: Change to **Bridal White**: 70 sc
Rnds 20–21: 70 sc (2 rounds)
Rnd 22: (3 sc, 1 dec) x 14 [56]
Rnd 23: 56 sc
Rnd 24: 1 sc, 1 dec, (2 sc, 1 dec) x 13, 1 sc [42]
Insert the Eyes between rounds 17 and 18 with 8 sc distance between them. Observe that there are two stitches in **Bridal White** color to each side.
Rnd 25: (5 sc, 1 dec) x 6 [36]
Rnd 26: 2 sc, 1 dec, (4 sc, 1 dec) x 5, 2 sc [30]
Rnd 27: (3 sc, 1 dec) x 6 [24]
Rnd 28: 1 sc, 1 dec, (2 sc, 1 dec) x 5, 1 sc [18]
Rnd 29: (1 sc, 1 dec) x 6 [12]
Rnd 30: 6 dec [6]
Stuff the Head before finishing off with the inverted magic ring.

EARS (MAKE 2)

With **Root Beer**, make a magic ring.
Rnd 1: 6 sc in ring
Rnd 2: (1 sc, 1 inc) x 3 [9]
Rnd 3: 9 sc
Rnd 4: (2 sc, 1 inc) x 3 [12]
Rnd 5: (3 sc, 1 inc) x 5 [15]
Rnd 6: 2 sc, 1 inc, (4 sc, 1 inc) x 2, 2 sc [18]
Rnds 7–8: 18 sc (2 rounds)
Do not stuff the Ears.
Pinch closed the Ear opening and crochet 9 sc to close it.
Leave a long thread to sew.
Pinch the closed part of the Ear in half and sew the Ears between rounds 7 and 8 of the Head.

ANTLERS (MAKE 2)

With **Chocolate**, make a magic ring.

Rnd 1: 6 sc in ring

Rnd 2: (1 sc, 1 inc) x 3 [9]

Rnd 3: 9 sc

Rnd 4: 3 hdc in the same stitch, 8 sc [11]

Rnd 5: 3 hdc, 8 sc [11]

Rnd 6: 1 dec triple, 8 sc [9]

Rnd 7: 3 hdc in the same stitch, 8 sc [11]

Rnd 8: 3 hdc, 8 sc [11]

Rnd 9: 1 dec triple, 8 sc [9]

Rnds 10–11: 9 sc (2 rounds)

Stuff the Antlers and leave a long thread to sew. Sew the pieces between rounds 4 and 5 of the Head.

MUZZLE

With **Bridal White**.

Work around the foundation chains. Start with 5 chains and from the second chain from the hook:

Rnd 1: 3 sc, 3 sc tog, 2 sc, 1 inc [10]

Rnd 2: 1 inc, 2 sc, 3 inc, 2 sc, 2 inc [16]

Rnds 3–4: 16 sc [16] (2 rounds)

Leave a long thread to sew. Insert the Muzzle between rounds 2 and 3.

Sew the Muzzle to the Head between rounds 19 and 22 and stuff it before fastening off.

SCARF

With **Bottle Green**.

Start with 81 chains and from the second chain from the hook, make:

Rnd 1: 80 hdc, chain and turn

Rnd 2: 80 hdc

Finish off.

BODY

With **Root Beer**, make a magic ring.

Rnd 1: 8 sc in ring

Rnd 2: 8 inc [16]

Rnd 3: (1 sc, 1 inc) x 8 [24]

Rnd 4: 1 sc, 1 inc, (2 sc, 1 inc) x 7, 1 sc [32]

Rnd 5: (3 sc, 1 inc) x 8 [40]

Rnd 6: 2 sc, 1 inc, (4 sc, 1 inc) x 7, 2 sc [48]

Rnd 7: (5 sc, 1 inc) x 8 [56]

Rnd 8: 56 sc

Rnd 9: 3 sc, 1 inc, (6 sc, 1 inc) x 7, 3 sc [64]

From round 10 onward there will be many color changes. The color you work with is indicated before each part.

Rnd 10: (**Root Beer**) 26 sc, (**Bridal White**) 12 sc, (**Root Beer**) 26 sc [64]

Rnd 11: (**Root Beer**) 25 sc, (**Bridal White**) 14 sc, (**Root Beer**) 25 sc [64]

Rnd 12: (**Root Beer**) 24 sc, (**Bridal White**) 16 sc, (**Root Beer**) 24 sc [64]

Rnds 13–14: (**Root Beer**) 24 sc, (**Bridal White**) 16 sc, (**Root Beer**) 24 sc [64] (2 rounds)

Rnd 15: (**Root Beer**) (4 sc, 1 dec) x 4, (**Bridal White**) (2 sc, 1 dec) x 4, (**Root Beer**) (4 sc, 1 dec) x 4 [52]

Rnds 16–20: (**Root Beer**) 20 sc, (**Bridal White**) 12 sc, (**Root Beer**) 20 sc [52] (5 rounds)

Rnd 21: (**Root Beer**) (3 sc, 1 dec) x 4, (**Bridal White**) (2 sc, 1 dec) x 3, (**Root Beer**) (3 sc, 1 dec) x 4 [41]

Rnds 22–23: (**Root Beer**) 16 sc, (**Bridal White**) 9 sc, (**Root Beer**) 16 sc [41] (2 rounds)

Rnd 24: (**Root Beer**) (2 sc, 1 dec) x 4, (**Bridal White**) (1 sc, 1 dec) x 3, (**Root Beer**) (2 sc, 1 dec) x 4 [41]

Rnds 25–26: (**Root Beer**) 12 sc, (**Bridal White**) 6 sc, (**Root Beer**) 12 sc [30] (2 rounds)

Stuff the Body and leave a long thread to sew.

SKIN MARKS

Make the skin marks using French knots (see page 132) in **Bridal White**. You can make as many skin marks as you want and place them according to your taste.

FRONT LEGS (MAKE 2)

With **Bottle Green**, make a magic ring.

Rnd 1: 6 sc in ring

Rnd 2: 6 inc [12]

Rnd 3: (3 sc, 1 inc) x 3 [15]

Rnd 4–5: 15 sc (2 rounds)

Rnd 6: Change to **Root Beer**. BLO 15 sc

Rnds 7–13: 15 sc (7 rounds)

Slightly stuff the Front Legs (do not fill to the top of the piece). Pinch closed the opening of the Leg and crochet 7 sc to close it. Leave a long thread to sew.

Insert the hook into the loops formed by round 6, and with the **Peridot Green** color, make 15 sl st and fasten off.

HIND LEGS (MAKE 2)

With **Bottle Green**, make a magic ring.
Rnd 1: 6 sc in ring
Rnd 2: 6 inc [12]
Rnd 3: (1 sc, 1 inc) x 6 [18]
Rnds 4–6: 18 sc (3 rounds)
Rnd 7: Change to **Root Beer**. BLO 18 sc
Rnds 8–14: 18 sc (7 rounds)
Slightly stuff the Legs (do not fill to the top of the piece). Pinch closed the opening of the Leg and crochet 9 sc to close it. Leave a long thread to sew.
Insert the hook into the loops formed by round 7, and with the **Peridot Green** color, make 18 sl st and fasten off.
Sew the Front Legs between **rounds 25 and 26**.
Sew the Hind Legs between **rounds 10 and 15**, leaving them a bit diagonally.
To sew the Body to the Head, see the instructions on page 135. Wrap the Scarf around the neck.

HERBIE THE SNOWMAN

Why go out into the cold to build a snowman when you can create your own while being warm and toasty inside! Snowmen, with their jolly smiles and frosty charm, have always been beloved symbols of the holiday season. Herbie, with his charcoal hat, green scarf, and red mittens, brings to life the festive spirit of snowy days and cozy winter nights.

YARN

1 skein of each of these colors:

Fingering weight (#1 super fine) yarn, shown in Hobbii *Friends Cotton 8/4* (100% cotton, 174 yd. / 160 m per 1.75 oz / 50 g skein)

SCARF

112 Bottle Green

HAT

123 Charcoal

NOSE

30 Orange

HAT DETAILS/MITTENS

40 Tomato

Fingering weight (#1 super fine) yarn, shown in Hobbii *Friends Cotton 8/4 Mercerized* (100% cotton, 174 yd. / 160 m per 1.75 oz / 50 g skein)

SKIN

01 White

ARMS

12 Chocolate

Lace yarn (#0 lace), shown in Hobbii *Rainbow Lace* (100% cotton, 306 yd. / 280 m per 1.75 oz / 50 g ball)

EMBROIDERY

009 Black

Note: *Any standard black embroidery thread can be used.*

FINISHED MEASUREMENTS

WHOLE BODY HEIGHT: 5.10 in. / 13 cm
WIDTH: 2.75 in. / 7 cm
HEAD HEIGHT: 2.35 in. / 6 cm
HEAD WIDTH: 2.75 in. / 7 cm

HOOK

- US B-1 / 2.25 mm hook

NOTIONS

- Polyester stuffing
- Tapestry needle
- Removable stitch markers
- Straight pins
- Two buttons
- Amigurumi glasses or craft wire to create the glasses
- Pair of 12 mm safety eyes
- A piece of cardboard to place at the bottom
- Craft glue

GAUGE

Gauge is not critical for this project. Ensure your stitches are tight so the stuffing won't show through.

For more information on how to make Herbie, including tips, step-by-step pictures, and videos, scan this QR code!

HEAD

With **White**, make a magic ring.
Rnd 1: 8 sc in ring
Rnd 2: 8 inc [16]
Rnd 3: (1 sc, 1 inc) x 8 [24]
Rnd 4: 1 sc, 1 inc, (2 sc, 1 inc) x 7, 1 sc [32]
Rnd 5: (3 sc, 1 inc) x 8 [40]
Rnd 6: 2 sc, 1 inc, (4 sc, 1 inc) x 7, 2 sc [48]
Rnd 7: (5 sc, 1 inc) x 8 [56]
Rnds 8–9: 56 sc (2 rounds)
Rnd 10: 3 sc, 1 inc, (6 sc, 1 inc) x 8, 3 sc [64]
Rnds 11–22: 64 sc (12 rounds)
Insert the Eyes between **rounds 16 and 17** with **8 sc** of distance between them.
Rnd 23: 3 sc, 1 dec, (6 sc, 1 dec) x 8, 3 sc [56]
Rnd 24: (5 sc, 1 dec) x 8 [48]
Rnd 25: 2 sc, 1 dec, (4 sc, 1 dec) x 8, 2 sc [40]
Rnd 26: (3 sc, 1 dec) x 8 [32]
Rnd 27: 1 sc, 1 dec, (2 sc, 1 dec) x 8, 1 sc [24]
Rnd 28: (1 sc, 1 dec) x 8 [16]
Rnd 29: 8 dec [8]
Stuff the Head before finishing off with the inverted magic ring.
Using **White**, indent the Eyes of the amigurumi (more instructions on page 132).

NOSE

With **Orange**, make a magic ring.
Rnd 1: 6 sc in ring
Rnd 2: (1 sc, 1 inc) x 3 [9]
Rnd 3: 1 sc, 1 inc, (2 sc, 1 inc) x 2, 1 sc [12]
Rnd 4: 12 sc
Rnd 5: (3 sc, 1 inc) x 3 [15]
Finish off and leave a long thread to sew. Slightly stuff the Nose and sew it between rounds 16 and 21.

EYEBROWS AND MOUTH

With **Black** work a line of embroidery to make the Eyebrows two rounds above the Eyes, using the width of **4 sc** and height of **1 round**.
With **Black** make the Mouth **2 rounds** below the Eyes, using the height of **3 rounds** and width of **6 sc**.

BODY

With **White**, make a magic ring.
Rnd 1: 8 sc in ring
Rnd 2: 8 inc [16]
Rnd 3: (1 sc, 1 inc) x 8 [24]
Rnd 4: 1 sc, 1 inc, (2 sc, 1 inc) x 7, 1 sc [32]
Rnd 5: (3 sc, 1 inc) x 8 [40]
Rnd 6: 2 sc, 1 inc, (4 sc, 1 inc) x 7, 2 sc [48]
Rnd 7: BLO 48 sc
Rnd 8: (5 sc, 1 inc) x 8 [56]
Rnd 9: 56 sc
Rnd 10: 3 sc, 1 inc, (6 sc, 1 inc) x 7, 3 sc [64]
Rnds 11–18: 64 sc (8 rounds)
Rnd 19: 3 sc, 1 dec, (6 sc, 1 dec) x 7, 3 sc [56]
Rnds 20–23: 56 sc (4 rounds)
Rnd 24: (5 sc, 1 dec) x 8 [48]
Rnd 25: 48 sc
Rnd 26: 2 sc, 1 dec, (4 sc, 1 dec) x 7, 2 sc [40]
Rnd 27: 40 sc

Rnd 28: (3 sc, 1 dec) x 8 [32]

Place a round piece of cardboard at the bottom, or any hard material to make your Snowman stand steady.

Stuff the Body and leave a long thread for sewing.

ARMS (MAKE 2)

With **Tomato**, make a magic ring.

Rnd 1: 6 sc in ring

Rnd 2: (1 sc, 1 inc) x 3 [9]

Rnd 3: 8 sc, 3 Dc in the same st [11]

Rnd 4: 8 sc, 1 dec triple [9]

Rnd 5: 9 sc

Rnd 6: Change to **Chocolate**: BLO 9 sc

Rnds 7–14: 9 sc (8 rounds)

Slightly stuff half of the Arms (until round 8) and leave a long thread to sew.

Pinch closed the Arm opening and sew it together with the remaining yarn.

Sew the Arms between rounds 25 and 26 with the thumbs facing up (the thumbs are the 3 Dc of round 3).

HAT

With **Charcoal**, make a magic ring.

Rnd 1: 8 sc in ring

Rnd 2: 8 inc [16]

Rnd 3: (1 sc, 1 inc) x 8 [24]

Rnd 4: 1 sc, 1 inc, (2 sc, 1 inc) x 7, 1 sc [32]

Rnd 5: (3 sc, 1 inc) x 8 [40]

Rnd 6: 2 sc, 1 inc, (4 sc, 1 inc) x 7, 2 sc [48]

Rnds 7–13: 48 sc (7 rounds)

Rnd 14: FLO: 1 sc, 1 inc (2 sc, 1 inc) x 15, 1 sc [64]

Rnd 15: (3 sc, 1 inc) x 16 [80]
Rnd 16: 80 sc
Finish off.

I-CORD

To make the colorful cord for the Hat and the Scarf, we will use the I-cord technique. See the instructions on page 136.

Make 1 piece of I-cord with **White** and **Tomato** to wrap around the Hat.

I made a 6.3 in. / 16 cm piece, but I strongly advise you to measure your piece around the Hat before fastening off.

Make another long piece of I-cord with **Bottle Green** to make a Scarf. Mine measures 23 in. / 58 cm, but I advise you to measure around the neck of the Snowman as you crochet.

ASSEMBLY

Place the two-color I-cord around the hat.

Sew the buttons to the front of the Body.

To sew the Body to the Head, see the instructions on page 135.

Wrap the Scarf around the neck.

PEPPER THE PENGUIN

Penguins, often associated with snowy landscapes and a fun-loving nature, bring a unique joy to Christmas celebrations. Pepper, with his festive scarf and earmuffs, symbolizes the warmth and togetherness of the season. In many holiday tales, penguins are depicted enjoying the festive cheer, reminding us of the joy found in simple, heartfelt moments.

YARN

1 skein of each of these colors:

Fingering weight (#1 super fine) yarn, shown in Hobbii *Friends Cotton 8/4* (100% cotton, 174 yd. / 160 m per 1.75 oz / 50 g skein)

HEAD/BODY

01 White

HOOD/BODY/WINGS

123 Charcoal

BEAK/FEET

26 Dark Yellow

Fingering weight (#1 super fine) yarn, shown in Hobbii *Friends Cotton 8/4 Mercerized* (100% cotton, 174 yd. / 160 m per 1.75 oz / 50 g skein)

EARMUFFS/SCARF

48 Dark Magenta

Fingering weight (#1 super fine), shown in Hobbii *Bohème Velvet Fine* (100% polyester, 208 yd. / 190 m per 1.75 oz / 50 g skein)

EARMUFF DETAILS

17610 Soft Rose

Lace yarn (#0 lace), shown in Hobbii *Rainbow Lace* (100% cotton, 306 yd. / 280 m per 1.75 oz / 50 g ball)

EMBROIDERY

009 Black

Note: *Any standard black embroidery thread can be used.*

FINISHED MEASUREMENTS

WHOLE BODY HEIGHT: 4.72 in. / 12 cm
WIDTH: 4.3 in. / 11 cm
HEAD HEIGHT: 2.75 in. / 7 cm
HEAD WIDTH: 2.75 in. / 7 cm

HOOK

- US B-1 / 2.25 mm crochet hook

NOTIONS

- Polyester stuffing
- Tapestry needle
- Removable stitch markers
- Straight pins
- Pair of 12 mm safety eyes
- Craft glue

GAUGE

Gauge is not critical for this project. Ensure your stitches are tight so the stuffing won't show through.

For more information on how to make Pepper, including tips, step-by-step pictures, and videos, scan this QR code!

HEAD

With **White**, make a magic ring.
Rnd 1: 8 sc in ring
Rnd 2: 8 inc [16]
Rnd 3: (1 sc, 1 inc) x 8 [24]
Rnd 4: 1 sc, 1 inc, (2 sc, 1 inc) x 7, 1 sc [32]
Rnd 5: (3 sc, 1 inc) x 8 [40]
Rnd 6: 2 sc, 1 inc, (4 sc, 1 inc) x 7, 2 sc [48]
Rnd 7: (5 sc, 1 inc) x 8 [56]
Rnds 8–17: 56 sc (10 rounds)
Rnd 18: (3 sc, 1 inc) x 14 [70]
Rnds 19–21: 70 sc (3 rounds)
Rnd 22: (3 sc, 1 dec) x 14 [56]
Rnd 23: 56 sc
Rnd 24: 1 sc, 1 dec, (2 sc, 1 dec) x 13, 1 sc [42]
Insert the Eyes between **rounds 15 and 16** with **7 sc** distance between them.
Rnd 25: (5 sc, 1 dec) x 6 [36]
Rnd 26: 2 sc, 1 dec, (4 sc, 1 dec) x 5, 2 sc [30]
Rnd 27: (3 sc, 1 dec) x 6 [24]
Rnd 28: 1 sc, 1 dec, (2 sc, 1 dec) x 5, 1 sc [18]
Rnd 29: (1 sc, 1 dec) x 6 [12]
Rnd 30: 6 dec [6]
Stuff the Head and finish off with an inverted magic ring.
With **Black** make the Eyebrows between **rounds 11 and 12**, using the space of **4 sc**.

BEAK

With **Dark Yellow**, make a magic ring.
Rnd 1: 6 sc in ring
Rnd 2: (1 sc, 3 sc in the same st) x 3 [12]
Rnd 3: 2 sc, (3 sc in the same st, 3 sc) x 2, 3 sc in the same st, 1 sc [18]

Rnd 4: 18 sc
Fasten off and leave a long thread to sew. Do not stuff the Beak.
Sew it between rounds 16 and 21 of the Head. Pass the remaining yarn between rounds 3 and 4 of the Beak to indent it and finish off.

HOOD

With **Charcoal**, make a magic ring.
Rnd 1: 8 sc in ring
Rnd 2: 8 inc [16]
Rnd 3: (1 sc, 1 inc) x 8 [24]
Rnd 4: 1 sc, 1 inc, (2 sc, 1 inc) x 7, 1 sc [32]
Rnd 5: (3 sc, 1 inc) x 8 [40]
Rnd 6: 2 sc, 1 inc, (4 sc, 1 inc) x 7, 2 sc [48]
Rnd 7: (5 sc, 1 inc) x 8 [56]
Rnds 8–13: 56 sc (6 rounds)
Rnd 14: 3 sc, 1 inc, (6 sc, 1 inc) x 7, 3 sc [64]
Rnd 15: 18 hdc, 12 sc, 1 hdc, 2 dc, 1 hdc, 12 sc, 18 hdc [64]
Rnd 16: 18 hdc, 12 sc, 1 hdc, 1 chain, 2 dc, 1 hdc, 12 sc, 18 hdc [65]
Rnd 17: 18 hdc, 12 sl st, 2 hdc, 2 dc, 1 inc hdc, 12 sl st, 18 hdc [66]–Finish off.

FEET (MAKE 2)

With **Dark Yellow**, make a magic ring.
Rnd 1: 8 sc in ring
Rnds 2–3: 8 sc (2 rounds)
Make one more piece repeating rounds 1 to 3. Join the two

parts with 1 sc. This will be the first sc of round 4.

Rnd 4: 8 sc, 1 sl st in the same st that started the round, 8 sc [17]

Rnd 5: 8 sc, skip the sl st, 8 sc [16]

Rnd 6: (2 sc, 1 dec) x 4 [12]

Rnd 7: (1 sc, 1 dec) x 4 [8]

Make 3 more sc to get to the end and close the Foot with 2 sc. Leave a long thread to sew.

BODY

With **Charcoal**, make a magic ring.

Rnd 1: 8 sc in magic ring

Rnd 2: 8 inc [16]

Rnd 3: (1 sc, 1 inc) x 8 [24]

Rnd 4: 1 sc, 1 inc, (2 sc, 1 inc) x 7, 1 sc [32]

Rnd 5: (3 sc, 1 inc) x 8 [40]

Rnd 6: 2 sc, 1 inc, (4 sc, 1 inc) x 7, 2 sc [48]

Rnd 7: (5 sc, 1 inc) x 8 [56]

Rnd 8: 56 sc

Rnd 9: 3 sc, 1 inc, (6 sc, 1 inc) x 7, 3 sc [64]

From round 10 onward there will be color changes to **White**. The color you work with is indicated before each part.

Rnd 10: (**Charcoal**) 26 sc, (**White**) 12 sc, (**Charcoal**) 26 sc [64]

Rnd 11: (**Charcoal**) 25 sc, (**White**) 14 sc, (**Charcoal**) 25 sc [64]

Rnd 12: (**Charcoal**) 24 sc, (**White**) 16 sc, (**Charcoal**) 24 sc [64]

Rnds 13–14: (**Charcoal**) 24 sc, (**White**) 16 sc, (**Charcoal**) 24 sc [64] (2 rounds)

Rnd 15: (**Charcoal**) (4 sc, 1 dec) x 4, (**White**) (2 sc, 1 dec) x 4, (**Charcoal**) (4 sc, 1 dec) x 4 [52]

Rnds 16–20: (**Charcoal**) 20 sc, (**White**) 12 sc, (**Charcoal**) 20 sc [52] (5 rounds)

Rnd 21: (**Charcoal**) (3 sc, 1 dec) x 4, (**White**) (2 sc, 1 dec) x 3, (**Charcoal**) (3 sc, 1 dec) x 4 [41]

Rnds 22–23: (**Charcoal**) 16 sc, (**White**) 9 sc, (**Charcoal**) 16 sc [41] (2 rounds)

Rnd 24: (**Charcoal**) (2 sc, 1 dec) x 4, (**White**) (1 sc, 1 dec) x 3, (**Charcoal**) (2 sc, 1 dec) x 4 [30]

Rnds 25–26: (**Charcoal**) 12 sc, (**White**) 6 sc, (**Charcoal**) 12 sc [30] (2 rounds)

Stuff the Penguin and leave a long thread to sew.

WINGS

With **Charcoal**, make a magic ring.

Rnd 1: 6 sc in ring

Rnd 2: (1 sc, 1 inc) x 3 [9]

Rnd 3: (2 sc, 1 inc) x 3 [12]

Rnd 4: (3 sc, 1 inc) x 3 [15]

Rnd 5: 15 sc

Rnd 6: 2 sc, 1 inc, (4 sc, 1 inc) x 2, 2 sc [18]

Rnds 7–11: 18 sc (5 rounds)

Rnd 12: 2 sc, 1 dec, (4 sc, 1 dec) x 2, 2 sc [15]

Rnds 13–14: 15 sc (2 rounds)

Rnd 15: (3 sc, 1 dec) x 3 [12]

Pinch closed the opening of the Wings and crochet 5 sc to close it. Leave a long thread to sew. Do not stuff it.

EAR MUFFS (MAKE 2)

With **Dark Magenta**, make a magic ring.

Rnd 1: 6 sc in ring

Rnd 2: 6 inc [12]

Rnd 3: (1 sc, 1 inc) x 6 [18]

Rnd 4: 1 sc, 1 inc, (2 sc, 1 inc) x 5, 1 sc [24]

Rnd 5: 24 sc

Rnd 6: Change to **Soft Rose**. (3 sc, 1 inc) x 6 [30]

Rnd 7: 30 sc–Fasten off.

Insert the **Dark Magenta** yarn at any stitch in round 7. Make 1 sl st and make 26 chains. Attach the chain with 1 sl st on the second Ear Muff and return making sl st in all the loops of the chains. Fasten off.

Note: I strongly advise you to measure the 26 chains in the Head of your Penguin and check if it is enough. Depending on your crochet tension, you might need more or less chains.

SCARF

With **Dark Magenta**:

Make 81 chains and from the second chain from the hook:

Rnd 1: 80 hdc, chain and turn

Rnd 2: 80 hdc–Finish off.

ASSEMBLY

Sew the Wings between rounds 25 and 26 of the Body.

Sew the Feet between rounds 8 and 14 of the Body.

To sew the Body to the Head, see the instructions on page 135.

Glue the Hood to Head.

Glue the Ear Muffs on top of the Hood and put the Scarf on your Penguin.

GUS THE POLAR BEAR

The polar bear crochet amigurumi pattern is inspired by the serene beauty of the North Pole and the magic of the holiday season. Polar bears, with their majestic presence and gentle nature, have become symbols of winter wonderlands and Christmas festivities. Although Gus's fur keeps him warm, he loves to don a cozy sweater and hat, to capture the feeling of cozy winter nights and festive gatherings.

YARN

1 skein of each of these colors:

Fingering weight (#1 super fine), shown in Scheepjes *Catona* (100% mercerized cotton, 136.7 yd. / 125 m per 1.75 oz / 50 g skein)

SKIN

105 Bridal White

Fingering weight (#1 super fine), shown in Hobbii *Friends Cotton 8/4* (100% cotton, 174 yd. / 160 m per 1.75 oz / 50 g skein)

SWEATER/HAT

87 Midnight Blue

Lace yarn (#0 lace), shown in Hobbii *Rainbow Lace* (100% cotton, 306 yd. / 280 m per 1.75 oz / 50 g ball)

SNOWFLAKES

01 White

Fingering weight (#1 super fine) yarn, shown in Hobbii *Friends Cotton 8/4 Mercerized* (100% cotton, 174 yd. / 160 m per 1.75 oz / 50 g skein)

CUFFS/COLLAR/POMPOM

17 Cognac

EYES/EYELASHES/MUZZLE

009 Black

Note: *Any standard black embroidery thread can be used.*

FINISHED MEASUREMENTS

WHOLE BODY HEIGHT: 6.3 in. / 16 cm
HEAD HEIGHT: 2.75 in. / 7 cm
WIDTH: 4 in. / 10 cm
HEAD WIDTH: 2.75 in. / 7 cm

HOOK

- US B-1 / 2.25 mm hook

NOTIONS

- Polyester stuffing
- Tapestry needle
- Removable stitch markers
- Straight pins
- One 1.5 cm safety nose in black
- Makeup blush (optional)
- Pair of pointy tweezers

GAUGE

Gauge is not critical for this project. Ensure your stitches are tight so the stuffing won't show through.

For more information on how to make Gus, including tips, step-by-step pictures, and videos, scan this QR code!

LEFT LEG

With **Bridal White**, make a magic ring.
Rnd 1: 6 sc in ring [6]
Rnd 2: 6 inc [12]
Rnd 3: 3 sc, 6 inc, 3 sc [18]
Rnd 4: BPsc 18 sc
Rnds 5–6: 18 sc (2 rounds)
Rnd 7: 6 sc, 3 dec, 6 sc [15]
Fasten off the first Leg.

RIGHT LEG AND BODY

Repeat rounds 1 to 7 for the Right Leg.
With the second Leg make 3 chains, and attach to the Left Leg with 1 sc. This will be the first st of the round.
Rnd 8: 15 sc, 3 sc in the loops, 15 sc, 3 sc in the loops [36]
Rnd 9: (5 sc, 1 inc) x 6 [42]
Rnd 10: 3 sc, 1 inc, (6 sc, 1 inc) x 5, 3 sc [48]
Rnd 11: 15 sc, (1 sc, 1 inc) x 6, 21 sc [54]
Rnds 12–16: 54 sc (5 rounds)
Rnd 17: (7 sc, 1 dec) x 6 [48]
Rnd 18: Change to **Midnight Blue**. BLO 48 sl st
Rnd 19: BLO 48 sc
Rnds 20–22: 48 sc (3 rounds)
Rnd 23: 3 sc, 1 dec, (6 sc, 1 dec) x 5, 3 sc [42]
Rnds 24–26: 42 sc (3 rounds)
Rnd 27: (5 sc, 1 dec) x 6 [36]
Rnds 28–29: 36 sc (2 rounds)
Rnd 30: Change to **Cognac**. 36 sc
Rnd 31: FLO 36 sc
Rnds 32–33: 36 sc (2 rounds)
Fasten off **Cognac** and bend the collar of the shirt.
Insert the crochet hook with the **Bridal White** in the first loop of round 31.

Make 36 sl st and leave a long thread to sew the Body to the Head.

With **White** embroider some snowflakes on the front part of the sweater and some French knots (see page 132).

HEAD

With **Bridal White**, make a magic ring.

Rnd 1: 8 sc in ring [8]
Rnd 2: 8 inc [16]
Rnd 3: (1 sc, 1 inc) x 8 [24]
Rnd 4: 1 sc, 1 inc, (2 sc, 1 inc) x 7, 1 sc [32]
Rnd 5: (3 sc, 1 inc) x 8 [40]
Rnd 6: 2 sc, 1 inc, (4 sc, 1 inc) x 7, 2 sc [48]
Rnd 7: (5 sc, 1 inc) x 8 [56]
Rnds 8–16: 56 sc (9 rounds)
Rnd 17: 16 sc, (1 sc, 1 inc) x 12, 16 sc [68]
Rnds 18–21: 68 sc (4 rounds)
Rnd 22: 16 sc, (1 sc, 1 dec) x 12, 16 sc [56]
Rnd 23: (5 sc, 1 dec) x 8 [48]
Rnd 24: 2 sc, 1 dec, (4 sc, 1 dec) x 7, 2 sc [40]

Insert the Nose between rounds 16 and 17. Observe that the Nose should be in the middle of the same line as the increase part made in round 22. To facilitate finding the middle of round 22, you can mark the first and the last increases of the round.

Start stuffing as you decrease the rounds. When stuffing, remember to put more stuffing in the front part to create the volume of the Muzzle.

Rnd 25: (3 sc, 1 dec) x 8 [32]
Rnd 26: 1 sc, 1 dec, (2 sc, 1 dec) x 7, 1 sc [24]
Rnd 27: (1 sc, 1 inc) x 8 [16]
Rnd 28: 8 dec [8]

Finish off with the inverted magic ring.

With **Black**, embroider the Eyes and Eyelashes following the instructions on page 132.

Embroider the Eyes and Eyelashes between rounds 14 and 15, 1 sc apart from the Nose. Observe that the width of the Eyes takes about 5 sc.

Embroider a vertical line from the tip of the Muzzle to 5 rounds below it, to complete

the Muzzle. If you want to make your Polar Bear look even cuter, you can apply some blush on his cheeks and inside the Ears.

TAIL

With **Bridal White**, make a magic ring.
Rnd 1: 6 sc in ring [6]
Rnd 2: 6 inc [12]
Rnd 3: (1 sc, 1 inc) x 6 [18]
Rnd 4: 18 sc
Rnd 5: (4 sc, 1 dec) x 3 [15]
Leave a long thread for sewing.

EARS (MAKE 2)

With **Bridal White**, make a magic ring.
Rnd 1: 6 sc in ring [6]
Rnd 2: 6 inc [12]
Rnd 3: (1 sc, 1 inc) x 6 [18]
Rnd 4: 1 sc, 1 inc, (2 sc, 1 inc) x 5, 1 sc [24]
Rnds 5–6: 24 sc (2 rounds)
Pinch closed the Ears and crochet both sides with 12 sc to close it. Leave a long thread for sewing.

ARMS (MAKE 2)

With **Bridal White**, make a magic ring.
Rnd 1: 6 sc in ring [6]
Rnd 2: 6 inc [12]
Rnd 3: 12 sc
Rnd 4: Change to **Cognac**. BLO 12 sl st
Rnd 5: BLO 12 sc
Rnd 6: Change to **Midnight Blue**. 12 sc
Rnds 7–11: 12 sc (5 rounds)
Put stuffing until the middle of the Arms. Pinch closed the Arms and crochet 6 sc joining both sides of the Arm opening. Leave a long thread for sewing.

CUFFS (MAKE 2)

With **Cognac**:
Insert the crochet hook in the loops from round 5. Place the Arms upside down and make:
Rnd 1–2: 12 sc (2 rounds)
Fasten off.

HAT

With **Midnight Blue**:
Start with 25 chains and from the second chain from the hook make:
Row 1: 24 sc, chain and turn
Rows 2–22: BLO 24 sc, chain and turn (21 rounds)
Row 23: BLO. 6 sc, 10 chains and skip 10 sc, 8 sc, chain and turn
Rows 24–47: BLO 24 sc, chain and turn (24 rounds)
Row 48: 8 sc, 10 chains and skip 10 sc, 6 sc, chain and turn
Rows 49–54: BLO 24 sc (6 rounds)
Position the piece in a way that the first and last rows are joined together, and then crochet both parts together with 24 sl st.
Now we have basically a cylinder and we want to shrink the top side as to look like a beanie. Cut a long piece of thread and pass this remaining thread in a zigzag on the rows, using only the top stitches (the ones on the top side of the cylinder). Observe that the larger part below the hole of the Ears is the down part!
Pull the thread to shrink the Hat and close it. Fasten off.
With **Cognac**, make a small Pompom to place at the top of the hat.
(You can find my video tutorial on YouTube on how to make the Pompom just using a fork!)

ASSEMBLY

Sew the Arms on the side of the Body, between rounds 28 and 29.
Sew the Ears on the Head between rounds 6 and 13, with the bottom part of the Ear separated 5 stitches apart from the Eyes, and the top part of the Ear 4 stitches back. Observe that the Ears should be curved.
Sew the Body to the Head.
Sew the Tail in the back, below the sweater.
Sew the Pompom on top of the Hat. Place the Hat on the Head.

SEASONAL CHARACTERS

THE NUTCRACKER

Inspired by the timeless charm of the Nutcracker ballet, this character embodies the elegance and strength of this beloved holiday tale. Nutcrackers have always been a cherished part of Christmas, symbolizing bravery and magic as they come to life to battle the Mouse King. With his fancy clothes and soldierly stance, this nutcracker captures the enchanting spirit of the story, adding a touch of classic Christmas magic to your holiday décor.

YARN

1 skein of each of these colors:

Fingering weight (#1 super fine) yarn, shown in Hobbii *Friends Cotton 8/4* (100% cotton, 174 yd. / 160 m per 1.75 oz / 50 g skein)

SHIRT

82 Prussian Blue

BOOTS/HAT

123 Charcoal

Fingering weight (#1 super fine) yarn, shown in Hobbii *Friends Cotton 8/4 Mercerized* (100% cotton, 174 yd. / 160 m per 1.75 oz / 50 g skein)

SKIN

04 Cream

HAIR/MUSTACHE

01 White

PANTS

42 Cranberry

Fingering weight (#1 super fine) yarn, Hobbii *Tencel Bamboo Fine* (40% Tencel, 60% bamboo viscose, 230 yd. / 210 m per 1.8 oz / 50 g skein)

GOLD DETAILS

17473 Curry

FINISHED MEASUREMENTS

WHOLE BODY HEIGHT: 5.5 in. / 16 cm
WIDTH: 2.35 in. / 6 cm
HEAD HEIGHT: 2.75 in. / 7 cm
HEAD WIDTH: 3.15 in. / 8 cm

HOOK

- US B-1 / 2.25 mm hook

NOTIONS

- Polyester stuffing
- Tapestry needle
- Removable stitch markers
- Straight pins
- Craft glue
- Pair of pointy tweezers
- Pair of 12 mm safety eyes

GAUGE

Gauge is not critical for this project. Ensure your stitches are tight so the stuffing won't show through.

For more information on how to make the Nutcracker, including tips, step-by-step pictures, and videos, scan this QR code!

HEAD

With **Cream**, make a magic ring.
Rnd 1: 8 sc in ring
Rnd 2: 8 inc [16]
Rnd 3: (1 sc, 1 inc) x 8 [24]
Rnd 4: 1 sc, 1 inc, (2 sc, 1 inc) x 7, 1 sc [32]
Rnd 5: (3 sc, 1 inc) x 8 [40]
Rnd 6: 2 sc, 1 inc, (4 sc, 1 inc) x 7, 2 sc [48]
Rnd 7: (5 sc, 1 inc) x 8 [56]
Rnds 8–17: 56 sc (10 rounds)
Rnd 18: (3 sc, 1 inc) x 14 [70]
Insert the Eyes between **rounds 16 and 17** with **7 sc** of visible distance.
Rnds 19–21: 70 sc (3 rounds)
Rnd 22: (3 sc, 1 dec) x 14 [56]
Rnd 23: 56 sc
Rnd 24: 1 sc, 1 dec, (2 sc, 1 dec) x 13, 1 sc [42]
Rnd 25: (5 sc, 1 dec) x 6 [36]
Rnd 26: 2 sc, 1 dec, (4 sc, 1 dec) x 5, 2 sc [30]
Rnd 27: (3 sc, 1 dec) x 6 [24]
Rnd 28: 1 sc, 1 dec, (2 sc, 1 dec) x 5, 1 sc [18]
Rnd 29: (1 sc, 1 dec) x 6 [12]
Rnd 30: 6 dec [6]
Stuff the Head before finishing off with the inverted magic ring.
Make the Nose **2 sc** away from the Eyes, using the space of **3 sc**.
With **Cream**, indent the Eyes (see instructions on page 136).
With **White** embroider the Eyebrows between rounds 12 and 13, using the space of **4 sc**. Embroider the eye contour on the outer corner of the Eyes.

EARS (MAKE 2)

With **Cream**, make a magic ring.
Rnd 1: 7 hdc in ring
Finish off and leave a long thread to sew.
Sew the Ears between rounds 15 and 18, and finish off.

HAIR

With **White**, make a magic ring.
Rnd 1: 8 sc in ring
Rnd 2: 8 inc [16]
Rnd 3: (1 sc, 1 inc) x 8 [24]
Rnd 4: 1 sc, 1 inc, (2 sc, 1 inc) x 7, 1 sc [32]
Now we will work around the 32 sc of round 4 to make the Hair strands.
St 1: 25 chains, and from the second chain make 24 Hdc, sc in the next st.
Sts 2–16: 31 chains, and from the second chain make 30 Hdc, sc in the next st.
St 17: 25 chains, and from the second chain make 24 Hdc, sc in the next st.
Sts 18–31: 1 Hdc [14]
Close with 1 sl st in the last st of the round.
You should have 17 strands of Hair.
The right side of the magic ring should face up.
Strands **1 and 17** are above the Ears and strands **2 to 16** are placed around the Head.
Pin everything before applying glue. Just a drop of glue in each strand of Hair is usually enough to secure it.
Roll the tip of each strand of Hair to create the curls.

MUSTACHE

With **White**.
Start with 14 chains and from the second chain make:
1 sl st, 1 hdc, 1 tr, 1 dc, 1 hdc, 1 sc, 1 sl st, 1 sc, 1 hdc, 1 tr, 1 dc, 1 hdc, 1 sc–Finish off the remaining thread.
Glue the middle part of the Mustache right below the Nose.

CAP

With **Charcoal**, make a magic ring.
Rnd 1: 8 sc ring
Rnd 2: 8 inc [16]
Rnd 3: (1 sc, 1 inc) x 8 [24]
Rnd 4: 1 sc, 1 inc, (2 sc, 1 inc) x 7, 1 sc [32]
Rnd 5: (3 sc, 1 inc) x 8 [40]
Rnd 6: 2 sc, 1 inc, (4 sc, 1 inc) x 7, 2 sc [48]
Rnd 7: (3 sc, 1 inc) x 12 [60]
Rnds 8–17: 60 sc (10 rounds)
Rnd 18: BLO 60 sc
Rnd 19: Everything FLO: 21 sl st, 1 sc, 2 hdc, 12 dc, 2 hdc, 1 sc, 21 sl st [60]
Finish off the remaining thread.
Position the Cap upside down. Insert the hook in the unworked loops from **round 18**, and with **Curry** make:
(1 sl st, 1 chain) x 60–Finish off.

CAP DETAILS

With **Curry**, make a magic ring.
Rnd 1: 6 sc ring
Rnd 2: 6 inc [12]–Leave a thread for sewing.
Make another piece from Rnd 1 to 2 and make 35 chains. Insert the crochet hook in the

first piece that you made and leave a thread for sewing.

Secure the Cap details with pins first.

When you have them in the desired position, sew the small balls between **rounds 8 and 9**, and leave the chains loose in the front part of the Cap.

ARMS (MAKE 2)

With **Cream**, make a magic ring.

Rnd 1: 6 sc ring

Rnd 2: (1 sc, 1 inc) x 3 [9]

Rnd 3: 8 sc, 3 dc in the same st [11]

Rnd 4: 8 sc, 1 dec triple [9]

Rnd 5: 9 sc

Rnd 6: Change to **Prussian Blue**: BLO 9 sl st

Rnd 7: BLO 9 sc

Rnds 8–15: 9 sc (8 rounds)

Stuff the Arms just a little and fasten off.

With **Curry**, insert the crochet hook in the front loops of round 6. Make:

(1 sl st, 1 sc) x 9–Finish off.

LEFT LEG

With **Charcoal**.

Working on both sides of the chains to create an oval shape, start with 5 chains and from the second chain:

Rnd 1: 3 sc, 3 sc in the last chain, continue on the other side of the chains: 2 sc, 1 inc [10]

Rnd 2: 1 inc, 2 sc, 3 inc, 2 sc, 2 inc [16]

Rnd 3: 1 sc, 1 inc, 2 sc, (1 sc, 1 inc) x 3, 2 sc, (1 sc, 1 inc) x 2 [22]

Rnd 4: BPsc 22

Rnds 5–6: 22 sc (2 rounds)

Rnd 7: 6 sc, (1 sc, 1 dec) x 3, 7 sc [19]

Rnd 8: 5 sc, 3 dec triple, 5 sc [13]

Rnds 9–12: 13 sc (4 rounds)

Rnd 13: Change to **Cranberry**. BLO 13 sc

Rnds 14–18: 13 sc (5 rounds)

Finish off and start again from rounds 1 to 18 to make the Right Leg (do not fasten off the Right Leg).

If you want your Nutcracker to have flat Feet to stand, make sure that you don't stuff it too much and leave it concave.

Before continuing the Body, let's make the details of the boot.

Insert the crochet hook in the unworked front loops of round 13. With **Curry**, make:

(1 sl st, 1 chain) x 13. Don't finish off.

Cut a long piece of thread to make the "X" shapes in the boot between rounds 8 and 9, and 10 and 11. Finish off.

RIGHT LEG AND BODY

With the Right Leg, make 3 more sc to get to the side. Be sure that both Feet are facing forward at the junction of the Legs.

Make 1 chain and fasten it with 1 sc on the first Leg. This will be the first stitch of the round.

Rnd 19: 13 sc in the first Leg, 1 sc using one loop of the chain, 13 sc in the second Leg, 1 sc in using the other loop from the chain [28]

Rnd 20–24: 28 sc (5 rounds)

Rnd 25: Change to **Prussian Blue**. 28 sc

Rnd 26: BLO 28 sc

Rnd 27–30: 28 sc (3 rounds)

***Rnd 31:** 6 sc, 9 sc joining the first Arm, 13 sc, 9 sc joining the second Arm, 9 sc [46]. The important thing here is that both Arms should be aligned on the sides of the Body. You might need to adjust the stitches accordingly.

Rnd 32: (21 sc, 1 dec) x 2 [44]
Rnd 33: (9 sc, 1 dec) x 4 [40]
Rnd 34: (2 sc, 1 dec) x 10 [30]
Rnd 35: (3 sc, 1 dec) x 6 [24]
Rnd 36: Change to **Cream**: BLO 24 sl st
Rnd 37: BLO (2 sc, 1 dec) x 6 (18)
Rnd 38: 18 sc–Leave a long thread for sewing.

TIP 1: I recommend you stuff the Body as you crochet. Using tweezers to stuff small parts like the Arms can be very helpful.

TIP 2: Making decreases using the back loops can be a bit tricky. Check the instructions on page 140 to learn how to do it.

CONTINUATION OF THE SHIRT

With **Prussian Blue**.

Position the Body upside down. Insert the hook in the last loop of round 26 and make:

Rnd 1: 28 sc
Rnd 2: 15 sc, chain and turn.

From now on we will work in rows, always making chains to turn.

Row 3: Skip 1 st, 25 sc, skip 1 st, 1 sc, chain and turn
Row 4: Skip 1 st, 23 sc, skip 1 st, 1 sc, chain and turn
Row 5: Skip 1 st, 21 sc, skip 1 st, 1 sc, chain and turn
Row 6: 22 sc

Make 1 chain and 4 sc, make 1 sl st in the middle part of the shirt and more 4 sc in the other side of the "V." Finish off.

COLLAR

With **Curry**.

Insert the hook in the front loops of round 36, and make: (1 sl st, 1 chain) x 18–Finish off.

BELT

With **Charcoal**.

Make 29 chains, and from the second chain from the hook make 28 sc. Leave a long thread for sewing.

Pin the Belt around the Nutcracker's waist and sew the Belt closed around the Body. Finish off.

With **Curry**, insert the tapestry needle into the Body. Pass the thread 4 to 5 times around the Belt to form the buckle. Return with the tapestry needle to the same gap where you first started. Tie a knot and push this knot inwards with the help of the tweezers.

FRONT PART OF THE BLOUSE (MAKE 2)

With **Curry**.

Make 7 chains and leave a long thread.

Pin both chains on the Nutcracker's chest.

With the tapestry needle, pass both ends of the chains inside the Body and tie a knot. You can leave these remaining threads inside the Body.

ARMS DETAILS (MAKE 2)

With **Curry**, make a magic ring.

Rnd 1: 6 sc in ring

Rnd 2: 6 inc [12]

Finish off and leave a long thread to sew. Pin both parts before sewing, making sure they are even.

Sew the Arm Details onto the Nutcracker's shoulders and finish off.

To sew the Head to the Body, see the instructions on page 135.

Your Nutcracker is ready! You can now either use the Head alone as a tree ornament or sew the Head to the Body to have the whole doll ready for your Christmas decoration!

REX THE MOUSE

Rex is inspired by the enchanting tales of Christmas and the beloved *Nutcracker* story. In the ballet, the Mouse King leads his army in a magical battle against the Nutcracker, but here he does not wish to fight; all he wants is to enjoy the holiday season with his friends. Dressed in a blue jacket with a gold scarf and hat, Rex is ready to add a magical touch to your Christmas.

YARN

1 skein of each of these colors:

Fingering weight (#1 super fine) yarn, shown in Hobbii *Friends Cotton 8/4* (100% cotton, 174 yd. / 160 m per 1.75 oz / 50 g skein)

SKIN

117 Light Gray

JACKET

89 Deep Ocean

FEET/HANDS/INNER EARS

51 Baby Pink

HAT/SCARF

13 Ochre

EYE CONTOUR

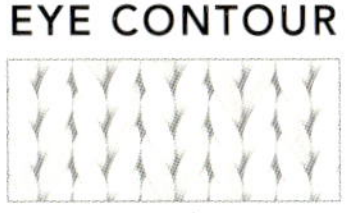

01 White

Lace yarn (#0 lace), shown in Hobbii *Rainbow Lace* (100% cotton, 306 yd. / 280 m per 1.75 oz / 50 g ball)

EMBROIDERY

006 Light Brown

FINISHED MEASUREMENTS

HEIGHT: 8 in. / 13 cm
HEAD HEIGHT: 2.75 in. / 7 cm
WIDTH: 3.5 in. / 9 cm
HEAD WIDTH: 2.35 in. / 6 cm

HOOK

- US B-1 / 2.25 mm hook

NOTIONS

- Polyester stuffing
- Tapestry needle
- Removable stitch markers
- Straight pins
- Craft glue
- Pair of 11 mm safety eyes
- One 1 cm safety nose in pink

GAUGE

Gauge is not critical for this project. Ensure your stitches are tight so the stuffing won't show through.

For more information on how to make Rex, including tips, step-by-step pictures, and videos, scan this QR code!

HEAD

With **Light Gray**, make a magic ring.

Rnd 1: 8 sc in ring [8]

Rnd 2: 8 inc [16]

Rnd 3: (1 sc, 1 inc) x 8 [24]

Rnd 4: 1 sc, 1 inc, (2 sc, 1 inc) x 7, 1 sc [32]

Rnd 5: (3 sc, 1 inc) x 8 [40]

Rnd 6: 2 sc, 1 inc, (4 sc, 1 inc) x 7, 2 sc [48]

Rnds 7–14: 48 sc (8 rounds)

Rnd 15: (5 sc, 1 inc) x 8 [56]

Rnds 16–19: 56 sc (4 rounds)

Insert the Eyes between rounds 12 and 13, 7 sc apart from each other.

Insert the Nose between rounds 14 and 15. Observe that the Nose should be in the middle of the Eyes.

Rnd 20: (5 sc 1 dec) x 8 [48]

Rnd 21: 2 sc, 1 dec, (4 sc, 1 dec) x 7, 2 sc [40]

Rnd 22: (3 sc, 1 dec) x 8 [32]

Rnd 23: 1 sc, 1 dec, (2 sc, 1 dec) x 7, 1 sc [24]

Rnd 24: (1 sc, 1 dec) x 8 [16]

Rnd 25: 8 dec [8]

Close the Head with an inverted magic ring and fasten off.

With **Light Brown**, embroider the Eyelashes, Eyebrows, and Muzzle.

With **White**, make the contour of the outer corner of the Eyes.

The inside part of the Eyebrows should be 3 rounds above the Eyes and the outer part 2 rounds above the Eyes, with a width of 4 sc.

ARMS (MAKE 2)

With **Baby Pink**, make a magic ring.

Rnd 1: 7 sc in ring [7]

Rnds 2–3: 7 sc (2 rounds)

Rnd 4: Change to **Light Gray**. 7 sc

Rnds 5–8: 7 sc (4 rounds)

Stuff the Arms just a little until the middle of the Arms.

Pinch closing it in and crochet 3 sc. Leave a long thread for sewing.

TAIL

With **Baby Pink**:

Start with 17 chains and from the second chain from the hook make:

Row 1: 16 sc

Leave a long thread to sew.

LEFT LEG

With **Baby Pink**.

Start with 5 chains. From the second chain from the hook, make:

Rnd 1: 3 sc, 3 sc in the same st, 2 sc, 1 inc [10]

Rnd 2: 1 inc, 2 sc, 3 inc, 2 sc, 2 inc [16]

Rnd 3: BPsc 16

Rnd 4: 16 sc

Rnd 5: 4 sc, 2 dec triple, 6 sc [12]

Rnd 6: Change to **Light Gray**. BLO 12 sl st

Rnd 7: BLO (3 sc, 1 inc) x 3 [15]

Fasten off the Left Leg and do it again from round 1 to 7 to make the Right Leg.

RIGHT LEG/BODY

With the Right Leg, make another sc to get to the side. The important thing is that both Feet are facing forward at the junction of the Legs. Don't put too much stuffing on the base of the Feet and leave them concave so the Mouse can stand on its own.

With the Right Leg, make 3 chains to join the Left Leg.

Rnd 8: 15 sc in the Left Leg, 3 sc in the chains, 15 sc in the Right Leg, 3 sc in the other side of the chains [36]

Rnd 9: (5 sc, 1 inc) x 6 [42]

Rnds 10–16: 42 sc (7 rounds)

Rnd 17: (5 sc, 1 dec) x 6 [36]

Rnds 18–20: 36 sc (3 rounds)

Rnd 21: 2 sc, 1 dec, (4 sc, 1 dec) x 5, 2 sc [30]

Rnds 22–23: 30 sc (2 rounds)

Rnd 24: (3 sc, 1 dec) x 6 [24]

Stuff as you crochet and leave a long thread to sew.

EARS (MAKE 2 EACH COLOR)

With **Baby Pink**, make a magic ring.

Rnd 1: 6 sc in ring

Rnd 2: 6 inc [12]

Rnd 3: (1 sc, 1 inc) x 6 [18]

Rnd 4: 1 sc, 1 inc, (2 sc, 1 inc) x 5, 1 sc [24]

Rnd 5: (3 sc, 1 inc) x 6 [30]

Fasten off.

With **Light Gray**, make a magic ring.

Rnd 1: 6 sc in ring

Rnd 2: 6 inc [12]

Rnd 3: (1 sc, 1 inc) x 6 [18]

Rnd 4: 1 sc, 1 inc, (2 sc, 1 inc) x 5, 1 sc [24]

Rnd 5: (3 sc, 1 inc) x 6 [30]

Do not fasten off.

Assemble the Ears by joining one **Light Gray** piece to one **Baby Pink** piece, repeat with the other pair. Place the **Baby Pink** and **Light Gray** pieces together facing each other. With **Light Gray**, crochet both parts together.

Rnd 6: 30 sc

Rnd 7: 2 sc, 1 inc, (4 sc, 1 inc) x 5, 2 sc [36]

Pinch closing just the tip of the round shape, to create the shape of a drop. Make 2 sc to create the drop and leave a long thread to sew.

ASSEMBLY

Sew the Arms on the side of the Body between rounds 23 and 24.

With the Ears, we are just sewing the tip of the "drop" that was formed. Sew this part between rounds 4 and 5, counting from the top of the Head, and 4 stitches back from the corner of the Eyes.

Sew the Tail in the back of the Body, between rounds 12 and 13.

HAT

With **Ochre**.

Start with 13 chains, and from the second chain from the hook make:

Row 1: 12 sc, turn

Rows 2–19: 12 sc, turn

Fold it in half and crochet both ends together with 12 sl st. Pass the remaining thread in zigzag in the stitches on the border and pull it. That way you shrink the top of the Hat. Bend the bottom of the Hat to make a cuff.

SCARF

With **Ochre**.

Make an I-cord piece with 4 chains in the base. To wrap the Scarf twice around the Mouse's neck, my I-cord measures 14 in. / 35cm, but you can make it any size you want. (See page 136 for instructions on how to make an I-cord.)

JACKET

With **Deep Ocean**.

Start with 31 chains and from the second chain from the hook make:

Rows 1–2: 30 sc, turn

Row 3: 3 sc, make 5 chains and skip 5 sc, 14 sc, make 5 chains and skip 5 sc, 3 sc, turn [30]

Rows 4–7: 30 sc, turn
Row 8: (5 sc, 1 inc) x 6, turn [36]
Rows 9–10: 36 sc (2 rounds)
Crochet sc around the Jacket. Make 10 sc on the sides, and 30 sc on the top of the Jacket (collar). Fasten off.

SLEEVES (MAKE 2)

With **Deep Ocean**.
Insert the crochet hook in the armhole opening created in the Jacket. Make:
Rnds 1–6: 12 sc (6 rounds)
Fasten off.
Dress your Mouse with the Jacket, Scarf, and Hat.

GINGERBREAD BOY

There is no more classic treat for the holidays than the gingerbread cutout cookies. This gingerbread boy is inspired by the sweet traditions of holiday baking. With his chef's hat, red tie, and candy buttons, he brings to life the magic of holiday kitchens and the warmth of family traditions. It is perfect for adding a delicious touch of charm to your holiday decorations.

YARN

1 skein of each of these colors:

Fingering weight (#1 super fine) yarn, shown in Hobbii *Friends Cotton 8/4* (100% cotton, 174 yd. / 160 m per 1.75 oz / 50 g skein)

SKIN

14 Caramel

STRIPES AND HAT

01 White

BOWTIE

40 Tomato

Lace yarn (#0 lace), shown in Hobbii *Rainbow Lace* (100% cotton, 306 yd. / 280 m per 1.75 oz / 50 g ball)

EMBROIDERY

009 Black

Note: *Any standard black embroidery thread can be used.*

FINISHED MEASUREMENTS

WHOLE BODY HEIGHT: 5.9 in. / 15 cm
WIDTH: 3.15 in. / 8 cm
HEAD HEIGHT: 2.4 in. / 6 cm
HEAD WIDTH: 2.4 in. / 6 cm

HOOK

- US B-1 / 2.25 mm hook

NOTIONS

- Polyester stuffing
- Tapestry needle
- Removable stitch markers
- Straight pins
- Three buttons / pebbles / polymer clay discs
- Pair of 12 mm safety eyes

GAUGE

Gauge is not critical for this project. Ensure your stitches are tight so the stuffing won't show through.

For more information on how to make the Gingerbread Boy, including tips, step-by-step pictures, and videos, scan this QR code!

HEAD

With **Caramel**, make a magic ring.

Rnd 1: 8 sc in ring

Rnd 2: 8 inc [16]

Rnd 3: (1 sc, 1 inc) x 8 [24]

Rnd 4: 1 sc, 1 inc, (2 sc, 1 inc) x 7, 1 sc [32]

Rnd 5: (3 sc, 1 inc) x 8 [40]

Rnd 6: 2 sc, 1 inc, (4 sc, 1 inc) x 7, 2 sc [48]

Rnd 7: (5 sc, 1 inc) x 8 [56]

Rnds 8–17: 56 sc (10 rounds)

Rnd 18: 16 sc, (2 sc, 1 inc) x 8, 16 sc [64]

Rnds 19–21: 64 sc (3 rounds)

Mark the **first** and **last** increases in round 18. This marking is very important to correctly position the Nose and the Eyes.

The Eyes should be placed in the middle of these increases in round 18.

Insert the Eyes between rounds 16 and 17, with 8 sc apart from each other.

Rnd 22: 3 sc, 1 dec, (6 sc, 1 dec) x 7, 3 sc [56]

Rnd 23: (5 sc, 1 dec) x 8 [48]

Rnd 24: 2 sc, 1 dec, (4 sc, 1 dec) x 7, 2 sc [40]

Rnd 25: (3 sc, 1 dec) x 8 [32]

Rnd 26: 1 sc, 1 dec, (2 sc, 1 dec) x 7, 1 sc [24]

Rnd 27: (1 sc, 1 dec) x 8 [16]

Rnd 28: 8 dec [8]

Stuff the Head before finishing off with the inverted magic ring.

Embroider the Nose between rounds 17 and 18, in the middle of the Eyes using the width of 4 sc.

With **White**, make the contour on the outer side of the Eyes.

With **Black**, make the Eyebrows 2 rounds above the Eyes, using the width of 4 sc and 1 round height.

COOKING HAT

With **White**, make a magic ring.
Rnd 1: 6 sc in ring
Rnd 2: 6 inc [12]
Rnd 3: (1 sc, 1 inc) x 6 [18]
Rnd 4: 1 sc, 1 inc, (2 sc, 1 inc) x 5, 1 sc [24]
Rnd 5: (3 sc, 1 inc) x 6 [30]
Rnd 6: 2 sc, 1 inc, (4 sc, 1 inc) x 5, 2 sc [36]
Rnd 7: (5 sc, 1 inc) x 6 [42]
Rnd 8: 3 sc, 1 inc, (6 sc, 1 inc) x 5, 3 sc [48]
Rnd 9: (7 sc, 1 inc) x 6 [54]
Rnd 10: 54 inc [108]
Rnds 11–14: 108 sc (4 rounds)
Rnd 15: 54 dec [54]
Rnds 16–19: 54 sc (4 rounds)
Fasten off.

ARMS (MAKE 2)

With **Caramel**, make a magic ring.
Rnd 1: 6 sc in ring
Rnd 2: 6 inc [12]
Rnds 3–4: 12 sc (2 rounds)
Rnd 5: Change to **White**. 12 sc
Rnd 6: Change to **Caramel**. 12 sc
Rnds 7–12: 12 sc (6 rounds)
Stuff the Arms, and then pinch closing them. Crochet 5 sc with both parts to close the Arms. Leave a long thread to sew.

BOW TIE

With **Tomato**:
Start with 21 chains and from the second chain from the hook make:
Row 1: 1 sl st, 8 sc, 2 sl st, 8 sc, 1 sl st, turn
Row 2–4: BLO (1 sl st, 8 sc, 2 sl st, 8 sc, 1 sl st), turn
Leave a *considerable* long thread. Sew both sides together, to close the Tie. Fold it in half, with the sl st in the middle of the piece. Wrap the yarn several times in the middle to form the Bow Tie and fasten off.

LEFT LEG

With **Caramel**, make a magic ring.
Rnd 1: 6 sc in ring
Rnd 2: 6 inc [12]
Rnd 3: (1 sc, 1 inc) x 6 [18]
Rnd 4: 18 sc
Rnd 5: 6 sc, 2 dec, 6 sc, 2 inc [18]
Rnd 6: 18 sc
Rnd 7: 5 sc, 2 dec, 6 sc, 2 inc, 1 sc [18]
Rnd 8: Change to **White**. 18 sc
Rnd 9: Change to **Caramel**. 4 sc, 2 dec, 6 sc, 2 inc, 2 sc [18]
Rnd 10: 18 sc
Fasten off.

RIGHT LEG/ BODY

With **Caramel**, make a magic ring.
Rnd 1: 6 sc in ring
Rnd 2: 6 inc [12]
Rnd 3: (1 sc, 1 inc) x 6 [18]
Rnd 4: 18 sc
Rnd 5: 6 sc, 2 inc, 6 sc, 2 dec [18]
Rnd 6: 18 sc
Remove the stitch marker and crochet 1 additional sc. This is where round 6 ends.
Rnd 7: 6 sc, 2 inc, 6 sc, 2 dec [18]
Rnd 8: Change to **White**. 18 sc
Remove the stitch marker and crochet 1 additional sc. This is where round 8 ends.
Rnd 9: Change to **Caramel**. 6 sc, 2 inc, 6 sc, 2 dec [18]
Rnd 10: 18 sc
Do not fasten off.
Join both Legs together to continue the Body. Make sure that when crocheting round 11, the Legs are arched out. You might need more or fewer stitches before joining the Legs depending on your crochet tension. The important thing to observe is that you crochet around both Legs (totaling 36 sc), make 1 sl st in the same st that joined the Legs (to avoid holes in the middle of the Legs), and that the Legs are arched out!
Rnd 11: 9 sc with the Right Leg, 18 sc with the Left Leg, 1 sl st in the same st that joined the Legs together, 9 sc in the Right Leg [37]
Rnd 12: 27 sc, skip the sl st, 9 sc [36]
Rnds 13–22: 36 sc (10 rounds)
Rnd 23: 2 sc, 1 dec, (4 sc, 1 dec) x 5, 2 sc [30]
Rnd 24: 30 sc
Rnd 25: (3 sc, 1 dec) x 6 [24]
Rnd 26: 24 sc
Stuff the Body as you crochet and leave a long thread to sew.

ASSEMBLY

Sew the Arms on the side of the Body, between rounds 24 and 25.

Sew the Body to the Head.

Sew the Bow Tie in the center of the Body, between rounds 24 and 25.

Glue the three beads on the center of the Body.

Place the Hat on the Head.

GINGERBREAD GIRL

This gingerbread girl, in her lovely, frosted dress with red lace and candy buttons, is a beloved character in the world of Christmas confections. In a cozy holiday kitchen, she comes to life, dancing among sprinkles and sugar, bringing joy to all who see her. Her adventures are filled with the scent of ginger and cinnamon, reminding everyone of the magical moments spent baking with loved ones.

YARN

1 skein of each of these colors:

Fingering weight (#1 super fine) yarn, shown in Hobbii *Friends Cotton 8/4* (100% cotton, 174 yd. / 160 m per 1.75 oz / 50 g skein)

SKIN

14 Caramel

STRIPES AND WHIPPED CREAM TOPPING

01 White

HAIRBOW

40 Tomato

Lace yarn (#0 lace), shown in Hobbii *Rainbow Lace* (100% cotton, 306 yd. / 280 m per 1.75 oz / 50 g ball)

EMBROIDERY

009 Black

Note: *Any standard black embroidery thread can be used.*

FINISHED MEASUREMENTS

WHOLE BODY HEIGHT: 4.72 in. / 13 cm

WIDTH: 3.15 in. / 8 cm

HEAD HEIGHT: 2.4 in. / 6 cm

HEAD WIDTH: 2.4 in. / 6 cm

HOOK

- US B-1 / 2.25 mm hook

NOTIONS

- Polyester stuffing
- Tapestry needle
- Removable stitch markers
- Straight pins
- Pebbles / polymer clay disks
- Pair of 12 mm safety eyes

GAUGE

Gauge is not critical for this project. Ensure your stitches are tight so the stuffing won't show through.

For more information on how to make the Gingerbread Girl, including tips, step-by-step pictures, and videos, scan this QR code!

HEAD

With **Caramel**, make a magic ring.

Rnd 1: 8 sc in ring

Rnd 2: 8 inc [16]

Rnd 3: (1 sc, 1 inc) x 8 [24]

Rnd 4: 1 sc, 1 inc, (2 sc, 1 inc) x 7, 1 sc [32]

Rnd 5: (3 sc, 1 inc) x 8 [40]

Rnd 6: 2 sc, 1 inc, (4 sc, 1 inc) x 7, 2 sc [48]

Rnd 7: (5 sc, 1 inc) x 8 [56]

Rnds 8–17: 56 sc (10 rounds)

Rnd 18: (3 sc, 1 inc) x 14 [70]

Rnds 19–21: 70 sc (3 rounds)

Insert the Eyes between rounds 16 and 17, with 8 sc apart from each other.

Rnd 22: (3 sc, 1 dec) x 14 [56]

Rnd 23: 56 sc

Rnd 24: 1 sc, 1 dec, (2 sc, 1 dec) x 13, 1 sc [42]

Rnd 25: (5 sc, 1 dec) x 6 [36]

Rnd 26: 2 sc, 1 dec, (4 sc, 1 dec) x 5, 2 sc [30]

Rnd 27: (3 sc, 1 dec) x 6 [24]

Rnd 28: 1 sc, 1 dec, (2 sc, 1 dec) x 5, 1 sc [18]

Rnd 29: (1 sc, 1 dec) x 6 [12]

Rnd 30: 6 dec [6]

Stuff the Head before finishing off with the inverted magic ring.

Embroider the Nose between rounds 17 and 18, in the middle of the Eyes using the width of 4 sc.

With **White**, make the contour on the outer side of the Eyes.

With **Black**, make the Eyebrows 2 rounds above the Eyes, using the width of 4 sc and 1 round height. Make the Eyelashes from the top of the Eyes to 2 sc to the side.

ARMS (MAKE 2)

With **Caramel**, make a magic ring.

Rnd 1: 6 sc in ring
Rnd 2: 6 inc [12]
Rnds 3–4: 12 sc (2 rounds)
Rnd 5: Change to **White**. 12 sc
Rnd 6: Change to **Caramel**. 12 sc
Rnds 7–12: 12 sc (6 rounds)

Stuff the Arms, and then pinch them closed. Crochet 5 sc with both parts to close the Arms. Leave a long thread to sew.

HAIRBOW

With **Tomato**:

Start with 21 chains and from the second chain from the hook make:

Row 1: 1 sl st, 8 sc, 2 sl st, 8 sc, 1 sl st, turn
Rows 2–4: BLO (1 sl st, 8 sc, 2 sl st, 8 sc, 1 sl st), turn

Leave a *considerable* long thread. Sew both sides together, to close the Hairbow. Fold it in half, with the sl st in the middle of the piece. Wrap the yarn several times in the middle to form the bow and fasten off.

LEFT LEG

With **Caramel**, make a magic ring.

Rnd 1: 6 sc in ring
Rnd 2: 6 inc [12]
Rnd 3: (1 sc, 1 inc) x 6 [18]
Rnd 4: 18 sc
Rnd 5: 6 sc, 2 dec, 6 sc, 2 inc [18]
Rnd 6: 18 sc
Rnd 7: 5 sc, 2 dec, 6 sc, 2 inc, 1 sc [18]
Rnd 8: Change to **White**. 18 sc
Rnd 9: Change to **Caramel**. 4 sc, 2 dec, 6 sc, 2 inc, 2 sc [18]
Rnd 10: 18 sc

Fasten off.

RIGHT LEG/ BODY

With **Caramel**, make a magic ring.

Rnd 1: 6 sc in ring
Rnd 2: 6 inc [12]
Rnd 3: (1 sc, 1 inc) x 6 [18]
Rnd 4: 18 sc
Rnd 5: 6 sc, 2 inc, 6 sc, 2 dec [18]
Rnd 6: 18 sc

Remove the stitch marker and crochet 1 additional sc. This is where round 6 ends.

Rnd 7: 6 sc, 2 inc, 6 sc, 2 dec [18]
Rnd 8: Change to **White**. 18 sc

Remove the stitch marker and crochet 1 additional sc. This is where round 8 ends.

Rnd 9: Change to **Caramel**. 6 sc, 2 inc, 6 sc, 2 dec [18]
Rnd 10: 18 sc

Do not fasten off.

Join both Legs together to continue the Body. Make sure that when crocheting round 11, the Legs are arched out. You might need more or fewer stitches before joining the Legs depending on your crochet tension. The important thing to observe is that you crochet around both Legs (totaling 36 sc), make 1 sl st in the same st that joined the Legs (to avoid holes in the middle of the Legs), and that the Legs are arched out!

Rnd 11: 9 sc with the Right Leg, 18 sc with the Left Leg, 1 sl st in the same st that joined the Legs together, 9 sc in the Right Leg [37]
Rnd 12: 27 sc, skip the sl st, 9 sc [36]
Rnds 13–18: 36 sc (6 rounds)
Rnd 19: 2 sc, 1 dec, (4 sc, 1 dec) x 5, 2 sc [30]
Rnd 20: BLO 30 sc
Rnds 21–24: 30 sc (4 rounds)
Rnd 25: Change to **White**. (3 sc, 1 dec) x 6 [24]
Rnd 26: Change to **Caramel**. 24 sc

Stuff the Body as you crochet and leave a long thread to sew.

SKIRT

With **Caramel**.

Position the Body upside down and insert the hook in the first loop from round 20:

Rnd 1: 30 sc

Rnd 2: 2 sc, 1 inc, (4 sc, 1 inc) x 5, 2 sc [36]

Rnd 3: 36 sc

Rnd 4: (5 sc, 1 inc) x 6 [42]

Rnd 5: 42 sc

Rnd 6: 3 sc, 1 inc, (6 sc, 1 inc) x 5, 3 sc [48]

Rnd 7: Change to **White**. 48 sc

Rnd 8: Change to **Caramel**. 48 sc

Rnd 9: FLO 48 sl st

Fasten off.

WHIPPED CREAM TOPPING

With **White**, make a magic ring.

Rnd 1: 8 sc in ring

Rnd 2: 8 inc [16]

Rnd 3: (1 sc, 1 inc) x 8 [24]

Rnd 4: 1 sc, 1 inc, (2 sc, 1 inc) x 7, 1 sc [32]

Rnd 5: (3 sc, 1 inc) x 8 [40]

Rnd 6: 2 sc, 1 inc, (4 sc, 1 inc) x 7, 2 sc [48]

Rnd 7: (5 sc, 1 inc) x 8 [56]

Rnds 8–10: 56 sc (3 rounds)

Rnd 11: (1 sl st, 1 sc, 1 hdc, 2 dc, 1 hdc, 1 sc) x 8 [56]

Rnd 12: (1 sl st, 1 sc, 1 hdc, 2 inc dc, 1 hdc, 1 sc) x 8 [72]

Fasten off.

ASSEMBLY

Sew the Arms on the side of the Body, between rounds 23 and 24.

Sew the Body to the Head.

Sew the Whipped Cream Topping to the Head.

Sew the Bow to the Whipped Cream Topping between rounds 8 and 9.

Glue two Beads on the center of the Body. Use as many Beads as you want on the Whipped Cream.

GNOME

Some gnomes like to sit in gardens to bring good luck to planters, but this little gnome has come in from the cold to celebrate his favorite holiday! Christmas gnomes are sometimes mischievous, taking bites out of cookies left for Santa, drinking all of the egg nog, and trying to take a peek at the presents—so keep an eye on this little guy!

YARN

1 skein of each of these colors:

Fingering weight (#1 super fine) yarn, shown in Hobbii *Friends Cotton 8/4* Mercerized (100% cotton, 174 yd. / 160 m per 1.75 oz / 50 g skein)

BEARD

01 White

HEAD

04 Cream

SHIRT

09 Nougat

PANTS

112 Bottle Green

BOOTS

15 Walnut

HAT/MITTENS

42 Cranberry

Fingering weight (#1 super fine) yarn, shown in Hobbii *Friends Cotton 8/4* (100% cotton, 174 yd. / 160 m per 1.75 oz / 50 g skein)

HAT DETAILS

123 Charcoal

BUCKLE

28 Mustard

FINISHED MEASUREMENTS

WHOLE BODY HEIGHT: 5.5 in. / 14 cm

WIDTH: 2.75 in. / 7 cm

HOOK

- US B-1 / 2.25 mm hook

NOTIONS

- Polyester stuffing
- Tapestry needle
- Removable stitch markers
- Straight pins
- Pair of 12 mm safety eyes

GAUGE

Gauge is not critical for this project. Ensure your stitches are tight so the stuffing won't show through.

For more information on how to make the Gnome, including tips, step-by-step pictures, and videos, scan this QR code!

HEAD

With **Cream**, make a magic ring.

Rnd 1: 8 sc in ring

Rnd 2: 8 inc [16]

Rnd 3: (1 sc, 1 inc) x 8 [24]

Rnd 4: 1 sc, 1 inc, (2 sc, 1 inc) x 7, 1 sc [32]

Rnd 5: (3 sc, 1 inc) x 8 [40]

Rnd 6: 2 sc, 1 inc, (4 sc, 1 inc) x 7, 2 sc [48]

Rnd 7: (5 sc, 1 inc) x 8 [56]

Rnd 8: 3 sc, 1 inc, (6 sc, 1 inc) x 8, 3 sc [64]

Rnds 9–23: 64 sc (15 rounds)

Insert the Eyes between **rounds 17 and 18** with **8 sc of** distance between them.

Rnd 24: 3 sc, 1 dec, (6 sc, 1 dec) x 8, 3 sc [56]

Rnd 25: (5 sc, 1 dec) x 8 [48]

Rnd 26: 2 sc, 1 dec, (4 sc, 1 dec) x 8, 2 sc [40]

Rnd 27: (3 sc, 1 dec) x 8 [32]

Rnd 28: 1 sc, 1 dec, (2 sc, 1 dec) x 8, 1 sc [24]

Rnd 29: (1 sc, 1 dec) x 8 [16]

Rnd 30: 8 dec [8]

Stuff the Head as you crochet and finish off with the inverted magic ring.

NOSE

With **Cream**, make a magic ring.

Rnd 1: 6 sc in ring

Rnd 2: 6 inc [12]

Rnd 3: (1 sc, 1 inc) x 6 [18]

Rnd 4: 1 sc, 1 inc, (2 sc, 1 inc) x 5, 1 sc [24]

Rnds 5–6: 24 sc (2 rounds)

Rnd 7: 1 sc, 1 dec, (2 sc, 1 dec) x 5, 1 sc [18]

Finish off and leave a long thread to sew. Sew the Nose between rounds 17 and 22, between the Eyes. Stuff the Nose while you sew it to the Head.

ARMS (MAKE 2)

With **Cranberry**, make a magic ring.

Rnd 1: 8 sc in ring

Rnd 2: 8 sc

Rnd 3: 7 sc, 3 hdc in the same st [10]

Rnd 4: 7 sc, 1 dec triple [8]

Rnd 5: 8 sc

Rnd 6: Change to **Nougat**: BLO 8 sl st

Rnd 7: BLO 8 sc

Rnds 8–12: 8 sc (5 rounds)

Slightly stuff half of the Arms (until round 8). Pinch closed the Arm opening and crochet it together with 4 sc. Leave a long thread for sewing it to the Body.

BEARD

With **White**, make a magic ring.
Rnd 1: 6 sc in ring
Rnd 2: (2 sc, 1 inc) x 2 [8]
Rnd 3: (3 sc, 1 inc) x 2 [10]
Rnd 4: (4 sc, 1 inc) x 2 [12]
Rnd 5: (3 sc, 1 inc) x 3 [15]
Rnd 6: 2 sc, 1 inc, (4 sc, 1 inc) x 2, 2 sc [18]
Rnd 7: (5 sc, 1 inc) x 3 [21]
Rnd 8: 3 sc, 1 inc, (6 sc, 1 inc) x 2, 3 sc [24]
Rnd 9: 24 sc
Rnd 10: (3 sc, 1 inc) x 6 [30]
Rnd 11: 2 sc, 1 inc, (4 sc, 1 inc) x 5, 2 sc [36]
Rnd 12: (5 sc, 1 inc) x 6 [42]
Rnds 13–15: 42 sc (3 rounds)
Rnd 16: (5 sc, 1 dec) x 6 [36]
Rnds 17–18: 36 sc (2 rounds)
Rnd 19: 2 sc, 1 dec, (4 sc, 1 dec) x 5, 2 sc [30]
Do not stuff the Beard. Pinch the Beard opening closed and crochet 15 sc closing the piece. Leave a long thread to sew it to the Head.

RIGHT LEG

With **Walnut**.
Working around the foundation chains. Start with 6 chains, and from the second chain from the hook make:
Rnd 1: 4 sc, 5 sc tog, 3 sc, 5 sc tog [17]
Rnd 2: 4 sc, 5 inc, 3 sc, 5 inc [27]
Rnd 3: (8 sc, 1 inc) x 3 [30]
Rnd 4: 30 BPsc
Rnds 5–7: 30 sc (3 rounds)
Rnd 8: 4 sc, 5 dec, 16 sc [25]
Rnd 9: 2 sc, 5 dec, 13 sc [20]
Rnds 10–11: 20 sc (2 rounds)
Rnd 12: Change to **Bottle Green**. BLO 20 sc
Rnd 13: 20 sc
Fasten off.

LEFT LEG AND BODY

Make the second Leg repeating the instructions from Rnd 1 to Rnd 13.
Before joining both Legs, with **Walnut**, insert the crochet hook in the first loop formed in round 12. Make 20 sl st and fasten off.
After finishing round 13, make 1 chain and attach it with 1 sc to the Right Leg. Make sure that both Feet are facing forward when you join both Legs together.
Rnd 14: 20 sc in the Right Leg, 1 sc in the chain, 20 sc in the Left Leg, 1 sc in the chain [42]
Rnds 15–17: 42 sc (3 rounds)
Rnd 18: Change to **Nougat**. BLO 42 sc.
Rnd 19: 3 sc, 1 inc, (6 sc, 1 inc) x 5, 3 sc [48]
Rnds 20–23: 48 sc (4 rounds)
Rnd 24: 3 sc, 1 dec, (6 sc, 1 dec) x 5, 3 sc [42]
Rnd 25: 42 sc
Rnd 26: (5 sc, 1 dec) x 6 [36]
Rnd 27: 36
Rnd 28: Change to **Cream**. BLO 36 sc.
Stuff it as you crochet and leave a long thread to sew.

HAT

With **Cranberry**, make a magic ring.
Rnd 1: 6 sc in ring
Rnd 2: (1 sc, 1 inc) x 3 [9]
Rnd 3–4: 9 sc (2 rounds)
Rnd 5: (2 sc, 1 inc) x 3 [12]
Rnds 6–7: 12 sc (2 rounds)
Rnd 8: (3 sc, 1 inc) x 3 [15]
Rnds 9–10: 15 sc (2 rounds)
Rnd 11: 2 sc, 1 inc, (4 sc, 1 inc) x 2, 2 sc [18]
Rnds 12–13: 18 sc (2 rounds)
Rnd 14: (5 sc, 1 inc) x 3 [21]
Rnds 15–16: 21 sc (2 rounds)
Rnd 17: 3 sc, 1 inc, (6 sc, 1 inc) x 2, 3 sc [24]
Rnds 18–19: 24 sc (2 rounds)
Rnd 20: (7 sc, 1 inc) x 3 [27]
Rnds 21–22: 27 sc (2 rounds)
Rnd 23: 4 sc, 1 inc, (8 sc, 1 inc) x 2, 4 sc [30]
Rnds 24–25: 30 sc (2 rounds)
Rnd 26: (9 sc, 1 inc) x 3 [33]
Rnds 27–28: 33 sc (2 rounds)
Rnd 29: 5 sc, 1 inc, (10 sc, 1 inc) x 2, 5 sc [36]
Rnds 30–31: 36 sc (2 rounds)
Rnd 32: (11 sc, 1 inc) x 3 [39]
Rnds 33–34: 39 sc (2 rounds)

Rnd 35: 6 sc, 1 inc, (12 sc, 1 inc) x 2, 6 sc [42]
Rnds 36–37: 42 sc (2 rounds)
Rnd 38: (13 sc, 1 inc) x 3 [45]
Rnds 39–40: 45 sc (2 rounds)
Rnd 41: 7 sc, 1 inc, (14 sc, 1 inc) x 2, 7 sc [48]
Rnds 42–43: 48 sc (2 rounds)
Rnd 44: (15 sc, 1 inc) x 3 [51]
Rnds 45–46: 51 sc (2 rounds)
Rnd 47: 8 sc, 1 inc, (16 sc, 1 inc) x 2, 8 sc [54]
Rnds 48–49: 54 sc (2 rounds)
Rnd 50: (17 sc, 1 inc) x 3 [57]
Rnds 51–52: 57 sc (2 rounds)
Rnd 53: 9 sc, 1 inc, (18 sc, 1 inc) x 2, 9 sc [60]
Rnds 54–55: 60 sc (2 rounds)
Rnd 56: (19 sc, 1 inc) x 3 [63]
Rnds 57–58: 63 sc (2 rounds)
Rnd 59: 10 sc, 1 inc, (20 sc, 1 inc) x 2, 10 sc [66]
Rnd 60: 66 sc
Rnd 61: Change to **Charcoal**. BLO 66 sl st
Rnd 62: BLO 66 sc
Rnd 63: 66 sc
Rnd 64: Change to **Cranberry**. BLO 66 sl st
Rnd 65: BLO 66 sc
Rnd 66: 5 sc, 1 inc, (10 sc, 1 inc) x 5, 5 sc [72]
Rnd 67: (11 sc, 1 inc) x 6 [78]
Rnd 68: 6 sc, 1 inc, (12 sc, 1 inc) x 5, 6 sc [84]
Rnd 69: 84 sc
Rnd 70: 84 sl st
Fasten off.
Using a tapestry needle and **Mustard**, make a buckle in the **Charcoal** part of the Hat (rounds 62 and 63), using the width of 4 sc.

ASSEMBLY

Sew the Arms on the side of the Body, between rounds 25 and 26.
Sew the Head to the Body.
Sew the Beard right below the Nose, between rounds 22 and 23.

TIPS, TRICKS, and TECHNIQUES

BEFORE YOU BEGIN

Remember that the complexity of a crochet pattern can vary depending on individual experience. This book includes not only the pattern instructions but also helpful tips, step-by-step photos, and QR codes for additional guidance. As you progress through the projects, I may reference techniques introduced in earlier patterns.

Progress at a comfortable pace and refine your skills through practice. Beginners should start with simpler designs, repeating them as needed to gain confidence before tackling more complex projects.

In the world of amigurumi crochet, there are no hard rules. Over time, each crafter develops their personalized approach that suits their style and comfort.

Yarn and Crochet Hooks

For all the characters in this book, I opted for cotton fingering yarn paired with a 2.2 mm crochet hook. Cotton is a popular choice for amigurumi due to its ability to create sturdy and long-lasting toys, and it's my preferred fiber for these qualities.

Switching to a different type or weight of yarn and crochet hook will alter the size of your finished piece. For instance, using an acrylic, worsted yarn with a 4.0 mm crochet-hook size will result in a much bigger and fluffier toy compared to what is illustrated in this book.

When it comes to choosing the best crochet hook, keep in mind that your hook should glide smoothly through stitches without too much resistance. If your stitches are too tight it may mean that you are using a hook that is too small, and you may want to go up a hook size. On the other hand, if there are large gaps in between stitches, you may be using a hook that is too large, and you may want to go down a hook size.

US	Metric
B-1	2.25 mm
C-2	2.75 mm
D-3	3.25 mm
E-4	3.50 mm
F-5	3.75 mm
G-6	4.00 mm
7	4.50 mm
H-8	5.00 mm
I-9	5.50 mm
J-10	6.00 mm
K-10.5	6.50 mm
L-11	8.00 mm
M-13	9.00 mm
N-15	10.00 mm
P-16	12.00 mm

EMBROIDERY

The Backstitch

The backstitch is a simple, yet effective, embroidery technique often used for creating defined, durable lines, such as the Eyes on amigurumi. To perform a backstitch, start by pulling the tapestry needle and thread up through the fabric at your starting point. Next, make a small stitch forward. Then, bring the needle back up a stitch length ahead of your first entry point and pull it through. Finally, insert the needle back into the end of the previous stitch, working backward toward the start of your line. This process is repeated, creating a continuous, solid line that's ideal for adding expressive features like Eyes to your crochet projects.

How to Make Eyes and Eyelashes

Starting with the Left Eye, insert the pins for the shape of an arc and use them as a guide, as follows:

- The two upper pins are between rounds 13 and 14, 3 sc apart
- The two bottom pins are between rounds 15 and 16, 5 sc apart

Embroider the Eyes using the backstitch technique in the shape of an arc.

To make the Eyelashes, start on the side of the arc that is closest to the Ear, and embroider the distance of 1 sc to the side, and 1 sc to the upper diagonal.

To hide the remaining thread, see Fastening Off and Hiding Thread.

How to Give Eyes Dimension

Use white embroidery yarn to indent the Eyes of the amigurumi. Pass the tapestry needle through any stitch on the side of the piece to the bottom of the Eyes. Outline the Eye with the thread, inserting the needle into the top of the Eyes, returning with the needle to the same stitch where you started. Pull the two strands and tie a knot with them. The more you pull the strands, the more indented the Eye will be.

How to Make a French Knot

1. Bring the tapestry needle up through the gap between stitches.
2. Wrap the thread around the needle 3 times.
3. Insert the needle back into the same point or close to where it first came out, ensuring that the thread stays wrapped around the needle.
4. Gently pull the needle through to form the knot, keeping the wraps tight against the crochet piece.

Fastening Off and Hiding Thread

To hide the remaining thread whenever you are sewing or embroidering, I use two techniques:

1. Invisible knot: Using the yarn in the same color, grab on loop of any stitch next to where the yarn is. Pass the tapestry needle in it and tie a knot. Insert the tapestry needle again in the same gap close to where the yarn is, and pull it so the knot enters the amigurumi. Cut the remaining thread.
2. If there are two ends of the thread (when sewing the Ears for example): Insert the tapestry needle in the side of the Head and start embroidering. After you embroider the Eyes, go back with the tapestry needle to exactly the same place where you started and tie a knot. With the help of the tweezers, push the knot inside the amigurumi.

FINISHING YOUR PIECE

Stuffing Your Amigurumi

For most parts of the amigurumi, like the Head and Body, I recommend stuffing them as you gradually crochet. For some parts, there will be specific information regarding stuffing to achieve the correct result, like not overstuffing the Feet if you want your toy to stand on its own.

Stuffing significantly influences the final shape of your amigurumi, and finding the right balance is crucial. Overstuffing can make your toys appear bloated and stretch the fabric, causing the stitches to open. On the other hand, because polyester stuffing tends to settle over time, insufficient stuffing might lead to a deflated appearance eventually.

Tear the stuffing into smaller pieces rather than trying to stuff a big piece all at once. This will help keep it from looking clumpy.

Make sure the stuffing reaches into all of the corners and edges, so the piece will maintain the correct shape.

For smaller or narrower pieces, use the back end of your crochet hook or a pair of tweezers to push small amounts of stuffing where they need to go.

Gluing Your Amigurumi

In sections of your amigurumi that require gluing, opt for a craft glue that dries clear and is suitable for the materials you're working with. The quantity of glue needed will vary based on its strength, but generally, a small drop is sufficient. Be cautious not to over-apply, as excessive glue can seep out and damage the appearance of your finished toy.

Weaving in Ends

For pieces that are stuffed, you'll simply have to use your crochet hook to pull the ends to the inside of the piece. For pieces that are not stuffed, you will need to use your tapestry needle to work the ends back and forth through the nearby stitches to secure them in place before trimming them.

Crocheting Pieces Together

Many of the patterns in this book involve crocheting pieces together: Legs are crocheted with the Body, or the Vase is crocheted into the Tree. Be sure to crochet the pieces in the correct order so that you'll be able to attach them at the appropriate time.

Sewing Pieces Together

While many of the patterns in this book have elements that can be crocheted together, they all require a fair bit of sewing as well. Sewing crochet pieces together can be tricky and can have a massive impact on the final result, so it's important to set yourself up for success.

Always leave a sufficient length of thread for sewing—not too short to handle, but avoid cutting an excessively long piece that might lead to wastage.

TIP 1: Wrap the yarn twice to three times around the crochet part that you will attach. Ensure that it is not overly tight, which may cause it to be short. This length is usually enough to sew pieces together.

TIP 2: Use pins to keep the pieces aligned while you sew, which helps maintain the correct placement throughout the process.

When attaching the Body to the Head of the amigurumi, place the pins as indicated in the image. Pay attention to these details for seamless joints:

1. Insert the tapestry needle from the inside out, grabbing both loops of the stitch on the open part.
2. Push the needle perpendicularly into the adjoining piece—avoiding diagonal entries—and exit well below the next stitch you will work.
3. Pull the thread tight enough to make the seam invisible.
4. Make an invisible and very firm knot and hide all the ends inside the amigurumi.

This type of sewing can be used whenever you are sewing the Body to the Head, the Nose, or the Muzzle of the amigurumi.

How to Make an I-Cord

I-cords are usually flexible, so do not make your stitches too tight or use a smaller hook size to make them looser.

1. Put a slip knot on your crochet hook.
2. Make 2 chains.
3. Skip 1 chain and insert your hook into the second. You will now have 2 loops on the hook.
4. Wrap the yarn over and draw up a loop. You will have 2 loops on the hook.
5. Remove the second loop from the hook but make sure to not let this loop unravel while it's off the hook.
6. Wrap the yarn over and draw up a loop. Make sure to not pull the yarn through too tightly, or it will unravel the loop that's off the hook.
7. Return the second loop to the hook. Wrap the yarn over and draw up a loop. You'll have 2 loops on the hook.
8. Continue to repeat the steps until you've reached the desired length.

Always remember to avoid pulling the working yarn too tightly to keep your second loop from unraveling when it is off the hook.

Once you've reached the desired length, yarn over and draw through both loops. Weave in the ends.

How to Turn Your Amigurumi Figures into Ornaments

To convert the Head of an amigurumi into a charming ornament, start by cutting a piece of thread—approximately 8 inches (20 cm) long. Using a tapestry needle, thread it through the top of the amigurumi's Head. Securely tie the ends into a knot or bow.

This creates a loop that is perfect for hanging the ornament on a Christmas tree or elsewhere as a festive decoration.

For More Tips, Tricks, and Techniques

Scan this QR code for more instructions, videos, and other handy tips and content!

Resources

You can find the yarns used to crochet the characters in the book here:
Hobbii: www.hobbii.com/
Scheepjes: www.scheepjes.com/en/

STITCH ABBREVIATIONS

Stitch Abbreviations

1. Ch: Chain
2. Sc: Single crochet
3. Hdc: Half-double crochet
4. Dc: Double crochet
5. Sl st: Slip stitch
6. BLO: Back loop only
7. FLO: Front loop only
8. Inc: Increase
9. Dec: Invisible decrease
10. Sc2tog: Sc 2 st together
11. St: Stitch/stitches
12. Rnd: Round

The Single Crochet

Every character in this book is crafted using the X-shaped single crochet, also known as the "yarn under" technique. This method creates stitches that are tighter than those made with the V-shaped "yarn over" technique, resulting in amigurumi that are more compact and rigid.

US vs. UK Terms

This book is written using US terminology. If you are more familiar with UK terms, here is a helpful conversion chart:

US Terms	UK Terms
Sl st—slip stitch	**Ss**—slip stitch
Sc—single crochet	**Dc**—double crochet
Hdc—half-double crochet	**Htc**—half-treble crochet
Dc—double crochet	**Tc**—treble crochet
Sc2tog—single crochet 2 stitches together	**Dc2tog**—double crochet 2 stitches together

TECHNIQUES AND STITCH GLOSSARY

CROCHET AROUND A FOUNDATION CHAIN

Form the base of your project by making a chain of the desired length. To start crocheting in the round, insert your hook into the second chain stitch from the hook. Make sc according to the instructions of the pattern in both sides of the chains. Do not make sl st to join the rounds.

DECREASE USING BLO (BACK LOOP ONLY)

Normally, a decrease involves picking up the front loops of two stitches, but this method focuses on the back loops of the amigurumi. There are two possibilities to do that:

1. Insert the hook into the back loop of the first stitch, then into the back of the second stitch to form a "V" on the hook. Yarn over and make 1 sc.

2. Skip the next stitch entirely, tightening the yarn to avoid holes. (This is my favorite way of doing it!)

SLIP KNOT

Make a loop with the yarn. Insert your index finger and thumb through the loop and grab the working yarn (connected to the skein) and pull it through the loop, holding on to the tail. Pull until a knot is formed, insert your hook through the new loop and pull the working yarn to tighten the knot.

CHAIN (CH)

With a slip knot on your hook, yarn over and pull up a loop through the slip knot. Yarn over and pull up a loop through the loop on your hook. Repeat these steps as many times as the pattern calls for.

CRAB STITCH OR REVERSE SINGLE CROCHET

Instead of working from right to left as in regular crochet, the crab stitch is worked from left to right. Insert your hook into the stitch directly to the right of the hook (the last stitch completed). Yarn over and pull the working yarn through the stitch (you will have two loops on the hook). Yarn over again and pull through both loops on the hook.

MAGIC RING

Make a loop with the yarn, leaving a tail around 4 in. long. Insert your hook into the loop and while holding the loop steady, pull the working yarn through. Keep the working yarn loose while using your hook to grab the working yarn on the other side of the loop and pull it through the loop on your hook. Single crochet into the ring by inserting your hook through the large loop, yarn over and pull the working yarn through, yarn over and pull through both loops on the hook. Single crochet the number of stitches the pattern calls for into the magic ring and then pull the tail tight to close the ring. (If you do not like this method, you can also chain 2 and work the number of single crochet the pattern calls for into the second chain from the hook.)

SINGLE CROCHET (SC)

Insert your hook through both loops of the next stitch, yarn over and pull the working yarn through the stitch (2 loops on the hook), yarn over and pull the working yarn through both loops on the hook.

BACK POST SINGLE CROCHET (BPSC)

Insert your hook from back to front of the single crochet from the previous round.

Yarn over and pull the working yarn through from behind the post (you now have two loops on the hook). Yarn over again and pull through both loops on the hook to complete the stitch.

HALF DOUBLE CROCHET (HDC)
Yarn over, insert your hook through both loops of the next stitch, yarn over and pull the working yarn through the stitch (3 loops on the hook), yarn over and pull the working yarn through all 3 loops on the hook.

DOUBLE CROCHET (DC)
Yarn over, insert your hook through both loops of the next stitch, yarn over and pull the working yarn through the stitch (3 loops on the hook), yarn over and pull the working yarn through the first 2 loops on the hook (2 loops on the hook), yarn over and pull the working yarn through both loops on the hook.

SLIP STITCH (SL ST)
Insert your hook through both loops of the next stitch, yarn over and pull the working yarn through the stitch and through the loop on the hook.

BACK LOOP ONLY (BLO)
Work in the back loop of the stitch only: the loop that is farthest from you.

FRONT LOOP ONLY (FLO)
Work in the front loop of the stitch only: the loop that is closest to you.

INCREASE (INC)
Make 2 single crochet in the same stitch to increase the number of stitches by 1.

INVISIBLE DECREASE (INV DEC)
Insert hook through the front loops of the next 2 stitches, yarn over and pull the working yarn through both front loops (2 loops on the hook), yarn over and pull the working yarn through both loops on the hook (crocheting 2 stitches together to decrease the number of stitches by 1).

COLOR CHANGE
Color changes occur on the last stitch before the desired color will be used. Work the stitch in the old color until 2 loops remain on the hook, then use your hook to pull a loop of the new color through both loops. Tie the tail of the new color to the working yarn of the old color and cut the old color. If the color change occurs on the inside of a piece that will be stuffed there is no need to weave in the ends. If the color change occurs on a piece where the wrong side will be visible then weave in the ends securely.

RIGHT SIDE (RS)
When crocheting in the round, the right side is the outside of your project. If you are right-handed, you will be working counterclockwise, if you are left-handed, you will be working clockwise.

WRONG SIDE (WS)
When crocheting in the round, the wrong side is the inside of your project. You will know if you are working with the wrong side out if you are right-handed and you are working clockwise, or if you are left-handed and you are working counterclockwise. The patterns in this book are all written with the right side facing out; if you are working with the wrong side out, you will want to turn the piece so that it is right-side out.

ACKNOWLEDGMENTS

A big thank you to my editor, Karyn Gerhard, for your support and excitement throughout this process. The energy I felt from you after every meeting was unique and it boosted my creativity.

A special thanks to my husband, Eduardo, for your guidance, assistance, support, decisions, encouragement, and for always believing in me—even when I didn't believe in myself.

To my best friend, Fernanda, I can't thank you enough for being my emotional support through this whole journey and constantly reminding me to keep going.

A special thank-you to Edilaine, who helped me keep my sanity while writing both this book and my Master's thesis in Education. We both know this journey wasn't easy!

A big thanks to my brother, Bruno, for encouraging me when I left the Air Force to follow my dreams. You always believed in me, and that meant a lot.

Last but not least, thank you to my mom, Rosana, and my dad, Jose. I'm not only lucky to have you in my life, but God also blessed me with the best in-laws I could ever ask for. Thank you all for your boundless love and support.

ABOUT THE AUTHOR

Bianca is an amigurumi designer and craft lover who began crocheting in 2015 as a way to relieve stress from her former job as an Air Traffic Controller in the Brazilian Air Force. After years of crocheting as a hobby, she founded her business, Crocheniacs, which initially focused on selling finished amigurumi and later expanded to include her own original patterns.

A naturally timid artist, Bianca discovered a passion for sharing her knowledge with the crochet community through YouTube videos. Teaching others to crochet and spreading joy through each stitch and amigurumi creation brings fulfillment to her life.

She enjoys challenging herself with a variety of amigurumi designs, experimenting with different shapes, and exploring endless possibilities to bring her ideas to life. Bianca has published two amigurumi books, *Crochet Nativity* and *Funkogurumi*, which show a little of Bianca's range of ideas in the amigurumi world, reflecting her creativity and personal style. She holds a degree in Teaching Portuguese and English, a postgraduate certificate in English teaching methodology, and a Master's degree in Teaching, Learning, and Media Education from the University of Tampere, Finland. Alongside her experience as an Air Traffic Controller, she worked as an Aviation English Instructor for the Air Force. She also has a strong background in business, earning a spot at the European Innovation Academy through Tampere University. In her free time, she enjoys indoor climbing with her husband and cooking.

Website: www.crocheniacs.com
YouTube: www.youtube.com/@crocheniacs
Instagram: @crocheniacs

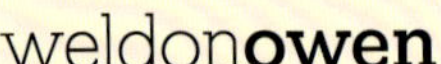

an imprint of Insight Editions
P.O. Box 3088
San Rafael, CA 94912
www.weldonowen.com

CEO Raoul Goff
SVP Group Publisher Jeff McLaughlin
VP Publisher Roger Shaw
Senior Editor Karyn Gerhard
Editorial Assistant Jon Ellis
VP Creative Chrissy Kwasnik
Art Director and Designer Megan Sinead Bingham
Production Design Jean Hwang
VP Manufacturing Alix Nicholaeff
Senior Production Manager Joshua Smith
Strategic Production Planner Lina s Palma-Temena

Weldon Owen would also like to thank B. J. Berti, Joanne Farness, and Dominik Sklarzyk for their work on this book.
Photography by Bianca Santos and Tytti-Kaarina Myöhänen
Author photo courtesy Gabrielle Dimer

ISBN: 979-8-88674-221-3

Manufactured in China by Insight Editions
10 9 8 7 6 5 4 3 2 1

Insight Editions, in association with Roots of Peace, will plant two trees for each tree used in the manufacturing of this book. Roots of Peace is an internationally renowned humanitarian organization dedicated to eradicating land mines worldwide and converting war-torn lands into productive farms and wildlife habitats. Roots of Peace will plant two million fruit and nut trees in Afghanistan and provide farmers there with the skills and support necessary for sustainable land use.